A gift for

_____

from

_____

Give it Forward

If You Received This Book as a Gift...

READ THIS!!

If you received this book as a gift, I ask that you keep the chain of giving going by giving this book as a gift to someone you care about, whether they be your family, friend or co-worker. Please read the next page, entitled *"Give Back by Giving Forward,"* to learn more about how you can help keep this vision going.

Buy 1 more

and

PASS IT ON!

Give Back by Giving Forward

In August 1998, as my path of spiritual growth was unfolding, I decided I was going to donate 10% of my income to a worthy cause. At the time, I was not comfortable with my options as to where my contribution would have the greatest impact so I asked my Higher Power for guidance on how to proceed. About a month later, the idea was presented – I was to invest my money, time and energy into publishing a FREE newsletter that would help raise the consciousness of people around the country. I was not to charge a subscription fee nor accept any advertising, as the newsletter's purpose was to be read, understood and *applied* by as many people as possible. This would be accomplished by keeping it FREE and limiting it to four pages, using only short stories so that even the busiest of us could read it.

The newsletter was started in January 1999, and as I write this, *"From Illusion To Reality – A Monthly Guide For Improving Your Life,"** is being read by thousands of people across the

---

* *See order form in back of book for information on how to subscribe to the newsletter.*

country. I knew that as time went on and the subscription base grew, I would be challenged to keep up with the ever-increasing costs but I was assured that the funds would always be made available as they were needed. This book is the culmination of the last two years of work that I've done as I've tried to share with others the concepts that have helped my life. Proceeds from this book will be used to cover the continuing monthly costs of producing and distributing the newsletter, allowing everyone their monthly spoonful of nourishment for their soul.

Many of my readers have been extremely grateful for the gift I've given them and have asked what they could do to give back. I always said when the time was right I would let them know. Well, the time is now right. I am asking each of you to *give back by giving forward*. What I ask is that you purchase one book for yourself to help fund the newsletter and buy one more and give it away to a loved one, such as a family member, friend or co-worker.**

Every one of us goes through challenges in life and many of your loved ones are going though their own right now. In my opinion, there is no better gift you can give someone than by touching that person's spirit with the light to help them through the challenges they may be facing. This book will certainly do that and you will be remembered forever because of it.

Mahatma Gandhi once said, *"Be the change you want to see in the world."* I'm doing what I can to help change the world one person at a time, now I ask you to do what you can to help me.

"Many people doing a little accomplish more than one person doing a lot."
- Andrew Moss

** *See order form in back of book for information on how to place your order.*

FROM ILLUSION TO REALITY
—BOOK 1—

A Simple Guide for Improving Your Life

ANDREW MOSS

INFINITY

PUBLISHING

Published by Infinity Publishing
6901 W. Okeechobee Blvd., #D-5/334
West Palm Beach, FL 33411

Back cover photo by Randy Hribko, Mort Kaye Studios,
    Palm Beach, FL
Design by Bookcovers.com
Edited by Linda Harter

Printed in the United States of America

ISBN 0-9713505-0-7

What people are saying about

FROM ILLUSION TO REALITY
— BOOK 1 —

"Thanks for all of your efforts on behalf of humanity."
Jack Canfield
Coauthor of the #1 *New York Times* best-selling
Chicken Soup for the Soul Series

"There is wonderful wisdom to be found here. Give yourself the gift of these insights."
Neale Donald Walsch
Author of the best-selling *Conversation with God* series

"FROM ILLUSION TO REALITY helps us to see the world from an expanded spiritual perspective. Andrew Moss has perfected the art of sharing spiritual messages in a simple manner that will inspire and enlighten his readers. His messages of love and compassion will lift your spirits and encourage you to also share and find your own personal truth."
Nick Bunick
Author of *In God's Truth* and *Transitions of the Soul*

"FROM ILLUSION TO REALITY has brought me great comfort. It has been one of the toughest years of my life…coping with my father's sudden death. At my lowest and darkest moments, I would reach for Andrew's words and always feel instant peace…a 'must-read' for everyone at every stage of life."
Kelley Dunn
News Anchor
NewsChannel 5, WPB, FL

"FROM ILLUSION TO REALITY is a wonderful book full of heartfelt and inspiring stories that serve as uplifting life lessons for all who read it. Andrew Moss shows us how to rise above human tribulation by realizing that there is always a higher power at work... knowledge that will change the reader forever. I highly recommend it!"

Michelle Whitedove
Author of *She Talks With Angels*

"Finally! A self-discovery book with real answers! FROM ILLUSION TO REALITY will move you toward positive changes in your life. A 'must-read' for anyone who wants to learn and grow!"

Lindy Rome
Radio Personality
SUNNY 104.3, WPB, FL

"Inspirational! Andrew Moss's work reflects a strong desire to raise the consciousness of humankind and to help us all explore our inner spirit."

Jill Chernekoff
News Anchor
FOX *Philadelphia*

"This book can serve as a wonderful vehicle to help people understand more about life. It touched a deep chord with me because of Northwood University's commitment to personal development, free enterprise and entrepreneurship."

- Dr. Arthur E. Turner
Founder
Northwood University

Contents

— Part 1 —
Tools for Life

— Part 2 —
Hidden Treasures

— Part 3 —
Miracles in Our Lives

— Part 4 —
Modern Day Parables

— Part 5 —
Ask Andrew

Acknowledgments

This book represents an extension of who I am and who I've become. There have been so many that have played a role in helping me open up and reach deep inside as I've traveled this path. Each one holds a special place in my heart and I am extremely grateful for the roles you have all played in my life.

First and foremost, I would like to acknowledge and thank my Higher Power who is with me always, guiding me through this journey, and truly is my best friend.

My Father, for leaving me with the greatest gift you could – unlocking the "door" to my true talent as you left to go "home."

My Mother, for always being there with your support and understanding.

My brothers, Manny and Alex, and sister, Marina, for the "building blocks of life" we played with as we grew up and became who we are now.

Eva Wyszynska, for being the one who helped me awaken to my true nature. Thank you for keeping our divine appointment and for sticking around until our work together was complete.

Brian Mylett, for helping me learn more than you could imagine and for allowing the Higher Power to speak through you and suggest doing the newsletter.

Mark Tosoni, for all of your support while I traveled this lonely, uncharted path and for lending an ear when I needed one.

Matt Kakuk, for running the show and demonstrating higher principles while I was "away at school."

Courtney Flower Haas, for helping me with the lessons we shared. I've grown tremendously as a result of them.

Mitch Schwartz and the Kingstar Foundation, for your assistance in reaching my readers every month.

Joanna Walker, for the time we spent when we first started this "class."

Dan Gewirtz, for demonstrating what friendship is really about.

Stephen Ziozis, for always being there for me when I was at the edge of the *"cliff of faith"* and providing solid ground under my feet.

Carolyn and Claudia Delk, for your ceaseless efforts for the newsletter.

Ann Pinto, for helping "spread the word" every Sunday.

Doc, for the "pop quizzes" and messages you unknowingly gave me on behalf of the Higher Power.

Tony Bruce, Peter Kanes, George Gounaris, Bob Preston, Mike Goldman, Jim McClafferty, Richard Blanc, Jihad El-Hassan and Frank Caputo for being in my life in your own unique ways.

I would like to send a very special thank you to Bob Canatta for having faith in my vision, the generosity of spirit and the courage to put the two together and make this book possible. Your funding allowed this book to go from being just an illusion to becoming a reality.

And for everyone else who has played a part in my life, even though you may not be mentioned by name, please know how grateful I am to have had the opportunity to experience a moment of life with you all and that I am a better person for it.

My Story

"Truth is what stands the test of experience."
- Albert Einstein

This chapter is the most important one of the book you are about to read because it will be the proof everyone is looking for <u>before</u> they take the risk of changing their lives by applying these principles. I've always had a strong desire to improve my life, and I know that so many others have that same desire. My desire brought these principles into my life, but before I could honestly share them with others, I wanted to make sure they weren't just words that sounded good and gave me comfort, but that they actually worked. Once I knew they did, it was my intention to share them with whoever wanted to listen. So for the past three years, I've dedicated my life to testing out these principles and demonstrating their validity. After you read my story, you be the judge and decide if they work. If you feel they do, I know you will not only read, but <u>study</u> the material that follows, knowing that if they worked for me, they will work for you as well.

Since I was a child, I've always been good with people and had an intense desire to help them, so much so, that I became a psychology major in college. After going through the courses that were offered, I lost my passion for psychology because the material just did not resonate with me. I then found out that I had a natural talent for sales. When I graduated from college, I started my sales career, but after a few successful years I realized that was not where I wanted to remain. Next, I went into sales management, and finally into ownership of a small sales company. I had climbed the small business corporate ladder all the way to the top and reached a level of success most of us would be happy to achieve. By that point, however, my life had become more complicated and I was experiencing challenges in all areas that forced me to look deep inside myself and decide if that was the direction in which I wanted my life to continue. It was because of those challenges that my desire to change became so strong and led me to open up to a force that I had not been familiar with on a first-hand basis. I had always believed in a Higher Power, or God, but for the first time, I felt a presence that was, in effect, a two-way relationship. I decided to explore this relationship and see where it led me. I started reading books to learn more about this Higher Power. This became my passion as I started to realize that it wasn't just about creating a better *after*-life for myself, but actually creating a better *present*-life. The more I learned, the more my passion grew and I slowly started to realize that my future was not going to be as I had always planned.

One day I was at a seminar being given by Dr. Wayne Dyer and he said something that changed my life forever. He said, *"If you don't love what you're doing, change what you're doing. Find a way to do what you love and the universe will find a way to support you."* I realized that I did not love what I was doing anymore and that it was time for a change. Within three months, I sold my company and left the business world. At that point, I had become financially successful, but by no means did I have enough money to retire. I had no idea what I was going to do with my life. Up to that point, I had a pretty

MARKET AMERICA
2002 INTERNATIONAL CONVENTION
JULY 25-28th

AMOUNT: $ 15.00

INITIALS: W.J.

Janet
Friday 2pm
Diane.

Isa Isha.

good idea of which direction my life would take, but it was becoming clearer to me that I was going to have to rewrite the script of my life because the old one was no longer valid. We all would like to have an idea of what our future holds for us, but now I was moving forward with no idea of what to expect. As I headed towards the unknown, this is what my inner voice told me:

> *"You will know what to do when the time comes. If you don't know what to do – do nothing. If you do something at that time, you're doing the wrong thing. Whatever you are searching for you will find without effort, in the most unexpected ways."*

That was to be my "flashlight" that would get me through the darkness of uncertainty.

As my brain was trying to figure out what my new path was going to be, God was telling me, *"I am your Source and I will not let you down."* I realized that I was being asked to go completely against what my brain was telling me and take a tremendous leap of faith and trust that I would be taken care of. At that point I had no idea what I was going to do but God left me with a small business that would run itself which would cover all of my living expenses, but no more than that, and that would free up my time to study and get to know Him on a much deeper level. It's as if my Father (God/Spirit) enrolled me at the "University of God" and was going to pay my tuition and living expenses and I was supposed to study and learn like I never had before.

As this was happening, my father's health began to deteriorate. At one point, he was in the hospital and I tried to call him but found out that his room had been changed and that he could not be located. I thought that was strange and figured there must be a reason I was not able to talk with him. Suddenly something shifted inside me and I was strongly guided to write him a letter. The moment I put the pen to paper, something started flowing out of me like never before. Writing had never been my strong point but his time it was effortless and when I was done I was amazed at the results. I wrote a story called "The Dream" (which appears on page 135) and when I showed it to my friends, they told me I had a gift and that I should pursue it. My dad passed away a few weeks later but I realized he left me with the greatest gift imaginable – on his way out of this world, he opened the door to my hidden talent; one that I never knew existed.

During my time of study, I knew it wasn't just about learning the principles but demonstrating them in my everyday life. Each month I focused on a different spiritual principle, such as love, patience, non-judgment, compassion, forgiveness, among others, until I was proficient at it. When the time came to demonstrate tithing, I decided to give 10% of my income back to God and a worthy cause. I did not feel right about any of the ideas that originally came to mind so I asked for guidance on how to give back. About a month later, in October 1998, the idea was presented that set off an "inner bell" letting me know that this was to be my path. I was to start a FREE newsletter that would help improve people's lives by spreading Higher Truths in a way that would be easy to read and understand and, therefore, implement. Principles would be discussed that were generally not taught to most people but that would allow them to experience the peace, health, and abundance they desired; and could be read by everyone, no matter what religion they belonged to. It was to be called *"From Illusion to Reality – A Monthly Guide for Improving Your Life."*

In this country, as well as the world, we have a crime problem, a drug problem, a poverty problem, an environmental problem, a moral problem, we have diseases that wipe out millions and the list goes on. We have grown accustomed to trying to heal the world by working on the *effects* but that will never work. In order to heal the planet we must work with the *SOURCE* of the problem. Our outer reality is created by what goes on inside of us – our thoughts and feelings. The ONLY way to change the outer is to first change the inner. I believe it is a process that will take time but it must start somewhere. I believe that if millions of people are reading information every month that helps them to change their thoughts and see things from a higher perspective, over time, that change will be guaranteed.

Within four weeks I had my first issue printed and the official start of publication was January 1999. When I thought about the prospect of putting out a monthly newsletter every month from then on, I became extremely anxious because I had no idea where the information would come from. When I had those thoughts, my Higher Self would put me at ease by telling me that God/Spirit was my source of the information and that I was just the channel that He was going to use to get the message out to humanity and that I should not worry about receiving the information. All I was to do was to allow the information to come through me and I would always have the information that I needed, when I needed it. I was also told that the newsletter was to remain FREE – I was not to charge a subscription fee and I was not to put in any advertising to help with the costs because they were only two channels that could be used to fund the project and that He had other ideas in mind. He promised me the costs would always be taken care of. The newsletter was to remain only four pages long, with each story being short enough to hold the reader's attention span or else it would not be read. The main goal of the newsletter was to deliver Spirit's message. In order to do that best it must remain pure – no advertising or fees. I was to allow Spirit to direct the current the growth of the newsletter would take. In the past, when I was in control, my idea was to grow as fast as possible. This time, however, He assured me there was a Divine timing in everything that was to take place and that I should use my intuition to stay with the current He set. That in itself took a tremendous amount of surrender, but that was one of the principles I needed to demonstrate. This was to be a co-creation with Spirit and He would be directing everything, especially during those times when I did not understand what was taking place. That would become important and would help me get through the next phase of my training.

The next phase started on Easter Sunday of 2000. I had

just come out of church after celebrating Easter morning services and went to check out the business that I had been running. I had always known that the business was a gift from Spirit and that it was on Spirit's time; whenever it was to end was up to Him. Little did I know that it would end abruptly on that Easter Sunday afternoon. With one phone call, I was informed that the business was being taken over by someone else. At that moment I realized that I was being told to "swim without the life preserver." I had grown enough and was now being told that I was able to create the money on my own using the principles I had learned. The business was the channel He had been using to bring the money to me and it was time to create a new one by tapping into the Source. It was extremely symbolic that all of this was occurring on Easter, and it was meant as a message for me. I was close to graduating from the "University of God" and it was time to demonstrate what I had learned. I would now be given the final exam.

As part of my "life preserver" was removed (my income), one part (my savings) remained. I had been tithing 10% of my income to the newsletter, but when my income was zero, I simply funded it using my own savings. I was now forced to live off my savings to cover my living expenses, as well as the expenses of the newsletter. At that point, I had enough money to last me two years, by which time I figured my book would be completed and generating a new channel of income for me. Part of me, though, saw what was to come. I knew that in order to truly float on faith, I would be required to lose the other part of my "life preserver." Well, that's exactly what happened. Most of my money disappeared in the stock market before it had a chance to be of any service to me. By January 2001, all of my money was gone, 12 months sooner than I expected with still no new income being generated. Of course, the fear of survival took over which led me to start looking for ways to create income. Every idea I came up with was denied. It was as if the universe was not allowing me to use my own efforts. Each time, my inner voice said I was to create it using the principles I had learned. I felt like Luke Skywalker in the movie Star Wars being told, *"Use the Force."* It was very frustrating, but I started doing exactly that.

The first thing I tried to create was the money I needed for a trip to Australia. I had been invited there to be in one of my best friend's wedding party but did not have the money to pay for the trip. It had been getting close to the deadline and he was waiting for an answer but I still had not manifested the funds to cover the expenses. I started following the advice I had been given which said, *"Create what you want as energy and essence. Let the form come to you in whatever way is best without focusing on what that form might be."* I was driving home from Orlando one Sunday night and decided I would do just that during my long quiet ride. I simply visualized being in Australia very intensely, feeling as if I was already there, without worrying about *how* the money for the trip would show up. Within 48 hours all the money showed up in the most miraculous ways.

When I got back from Australia, I realized I still had no money to cover my living expenses, which were pretty substantial. I was balancing my checkbook and had a balance of $13.51 left but then remembered that I had to subtract my monthly bank fee. I looked at the bottom of my statement to see how much it was and saw that it came to $13.50. I now had the grand total of **one cent** to my name!!! To make matters worse, my mortgage payment of almost $2,000 was now due. How was I going to pull off that one? I wrote the check and sent it in the mail knowing that my faith would have to create the funds before the check cleared. I decided to apply the same principles that created the funds for Australia. I knew that if I could create it once, I could create it again. I did my prayer work to create the money for my mortgage and surrendered it to the universe. There was nothing more I could do. A few hours later, a friend of mine from NY whom I hadn't spoken to in a few months called. He had no idea of the severity of my situation. He asked me if everything was okay. I said that it was and he said, *"I'm getting a funny felling that I should call you. Do you need any money, maybe $1,000 or $2,000?"* My jaw dropped in disbelief and I said, *"Yeah, actually*

I'm a bit tight. My mortgage is due and I could use some help." He said, *"How much is your mortgage? I'll send a check out today."* Once again, if I followed the principles and did the proper *inner* work, I would always be taken care of.

This is how it's been for the past three months as I've had to create the money to cover all of my expenses. Each time, even if it got down to the last second, I have always been provided for. This is the first time in my life that I've had a challenge with money. It represents an experience that I'm grateful to be going through because I'm seeing things that I would never have if I weren't going through it. I'm feeling tremendous support and understanding from my close friends and family. I'm able to experience the joy of humbly receiving help when it's given, which in the past would have made me extremely uncomfortable. It's also allowed my message to be more credible. You see, over the past few years, many people felt that my path was much easier than theirs and, therefore, I did not have the credibility that was needed to get the message across about the validity of these principles. They would say, *"That's easy for you, you don't have to work. All you do is read and study. You don't have the problems I have. That stuff may work great when you have no problems, but try living in my shoes and let's see how they work."* Well, the universe took away that objection by putting me through these challenges. Nobody can say I haven't had any challenges. I don't think many people could get through what I've had to get through without going insane. And more importantly, it's providing a lesson for others who have the chance, either first-hand or through this book, to see that if we apply these principles, we will always be taken care of, no matter how things may appear on the surface.

These challenges have represented a deeper test of my faith, as I have had to strengthen my faith beyond its previous limits in order to produce the miracle that we are all capable of creating. I've remained true to my vision, knowing that He would always provide for me. The Bible says, *"Whatever you ask for in prayer with faith, you will receive."* I have always asked Him with faith, knowing that He would provide the proper channel to continue my vision. As I write this, on Wednesday, April 4, 2001, I need to create $100,000 to fund the publishing of this book, which will start generating funds to live, as well as continue the newsletter. Once I learned a few weeks back how much money I needed for this project, I thought about borrowing the money from friends. That wouldn't be too difficult but I got a funny feeling that I was not supposed to do that; I was to create the money without asking anyone for it. I struggled with that idea because I could get myself out of this difficult situation within one week by borrowing the money and finally start living the way I had been accustomed to once again. This time, Spirit spoke to me in a dream in order to make Itself clear. Here was my dream:

> I was playing in the U.S. Open Tennis tournament and I made it all the way to the finals. I realized that I had broken a couple of strings on my racket so I tried to borrow some of the other players' rackets. Everyone I asked turned me down and I became very frustrated. I went to the equipment area and asked them for a new racket and they asked me who I was. I told them who I was and they said they never heard of me. I said, "I know, but after the finals, everyone will know who I am." They wouldn't give me another racket so I decided to use my own, even with the broken strings. I started walking to the court to play in the finals and then I woke up.

Here's what the dream means: The U.S. Open Finals represents the final exam that I'm going through right now. It then says nobody knows who I am now but after the Finals, everyone will. That tells me that after I get through what I'm going through and my book comes out, everyone will know who I am because the book will be very successful. Every time I asked someone for their racket I was refused, which means I'm not supposed to ask anyone for the money for this book; I'm supposed to "use my own racket even if a couple of strings are broken." In other words, even though I don't think I'm ready, I have the power to create $100,000. I was just supposed to apply the principles and visualize the $100,000 and not worry about how it was going to show up and it would be created without any outer effort.

This has not been easy. After three months of paying my bills this way, I have gotten pretty tired. Not knowing where next week's food is going to come from or how I'm going to pay my next bill can be extremely frustrating (although, to this point, I have always been provided for without ever having to ask anyone for help). Many times I've found myself feeling the pressure and getting impatient and thinking I should just try to borrow the money. So Spirit spoke to me in another dream.

> In this one, I'm driving down the road behind some other cars that are going at a normal pace. I'm in a big rush so I pass all of them. Next thing I know, I'm on the side of the road with four flat tires.

That's telling me that I must remain patient and stay in the flow that has been set for me because Divine timing is at work and if I step out of its flow, it will not work.

So, as I stand now, once again I have no money left. My book is done and waiting for the funds to publish it and I'm applying these principles ever so faithfully in order to create one last miracle that will allow me to pass this final exam.

It is now April 17th and nothing has shown up yet. I've managed to get through another two weeks, but I feel the pressure building and the walls closing in on me. I've had a few meetings scheduled with possible investors, but for some reason, all of them were postponed. I feel like I'm being teased; I see a light at the end of the tunnel but once I head in that direction the light goes out leaving me stranded in the darkness once again.

A good friend of mine called me last night because he was

experiencing the pain of going through a similar challenge. Whenever he feels this pain, he calls me because he knows I've already traveled the part of the path he's on now and he needs a little guidance to help him through. We had a great conversation and he got off the phone feeling much better. He called me this morning to thank me for inspiring him. I asked him what part of the conversation, in particular, inspired him. He said here I was, a guy with no money left and not knowing when or from where my next dollar is going to show up, going through one of the most difficult challenges one can face, and I'm about as positive and passionate as a person can be. He said he realized that it was because I had found and was following my passion.

And then it hit me...

My test is already over and it has nothing to do with the $100,000. I've already accomplished what I set out to do when I left the business world three years ago. I had no idea what I was supposed to do with my life at that time but I was told not to worry. I was to simply follow the path that Spirit would lead me down and everything would work out better than I could imagine. His words made me realize that I had been so focused on what I did not have ($100,000) that I did not notice what I did have. In the past three years I've unlocked a gift I never knew existed. I'm living my passion of helping people by sharing these principles, I have a newsletter that's read and loved all over the country and I have a book that is now complete. I can do what I want, whenever I want. I've gotten off the "roller coaster of life" and live in a world of peace and beauty, just as was promised to me in all the books I read. I am firmly entrenched in the present moment of a future that seemed to be so far away when I started this path three years ago.

So, what ever happened to the $100,000, you ask? You see, the moment I released my attachment to having it show up...it showed up. The fact that you're reading this book means that it showed up on its own Divine time.

And for those of you who wonder if God talks to us – the day after I received my check, I opened up a fortune cookie and it said the following: *"Don't forget, you are always on our minds. Congratulations!"*

Andrew Moss
Human Being
April 18, 2001

Opening Thoughts

"We live in a world of many illusions and much of human belief and behavior is ritualized nonsense."

"To a large degree 'reality' is whatever the people who are around at the time agree to."

"Your task...to build a better world," God said.
I answered, "How?...this world is such a large and vast place;
there's nothing I can do."
But God in all His wisdom said, "Just build a better you."

---

and so our journey begins...

An Owner's Manual for *"Your Life"*

W hen you buy a new car, it comes with an owner's manual that provides valuable information about how everything works. It explains all the details about many of the features you might not be familiar with. The cars of today are filled with so many new features but unfortunately many people never get to experience their benefits because they haven't read the manual. Its greatest value though is when there is a problem with the vehicle. At that point, you refer to it in order to help you solve the problem.

Think of this book as an *"owner's manual for your life."* It contains valuable information about many of the "features of life" you might not be familiar with, mainly because these things are not taught in today's society. Most of us are only using a few of the "features" that we have access to, simply because we've never had a manual that explained them in a simple and easy-to-apply manner. This book will identify many of these "features" and show you how to experience their benefits so you can enjoy "the ride" so much more. This "owner's manual's" greatest benefit though will be when you're going through a difficult challenge in life and you're experiencing pain. That happens to all of us and that is when life is the hardest because we seem so lost and it looks like there is no end to the pain in sight. When that happens, refer to this book because I <u>guarantee</u> you the ANSWER IS HERE.

As the saying goes, *"A smart man learns from his own mistakes, a wise man learns from the mistakes of others."* This book has been created because of the challenges I have gone through when I sorely desired a solution, as well as from observing others going through their own challenges. By applying the information in this book we become the "wise ones" as we "learn from the mistakes of others."

— Part 1—

Tools For Life

These "tools" can be applied to your life in order
to get out of any challenge, ease any pain, create
the life you desire, and see things from a higher
perspective and get a glimpse of "reality."

From Illusion to Reality

The One-Minute Solution

Everybody wants to improve their lives in one form or another. There is not one person who thinks, "My life is perfect, I don't want to improve a thing." It doesn't matter if we've attained the level of success we've always desired, we have all the money we thought we'd ever need, we have the family life we've always wanted or accomplished a specific goal we hoped to reach. There is always some part of our lives that needs improvement. We all know what areas we'd like to improve. Some of us realize there are <u>many</u> aspects of our lives we'd like to enhance; the question is "How?"

The first thing we have to understand is this: *For things to change, we have to change. For things to get better, we have to get better.* So how can we *"get better?"*

We must find the areas of our lives we would like to improve and make a conscious effort to change those areas. That means we must take the first step. I've heard all types of excuses why people cannot improve their lives, such as, *"I'm too busy, I don't have the time, I work too many hours, I have to raise the kids and I never get a moment alone, etc."* Understand this – ALL EXCUSES ARE EQUAL – THEY DON'T MATTER!!! Time alone does not solve our problems; it also takes effort. Avoiding the effort that is required to solve our problems will keep them anchored in our lives. Over the course of time, it will take more effort to deal with the problem than it will to solve it. What if I told you that before certain problems could be solved, you'd have to take certain simple steps and those steps would require only one minute everyday, and if you didn't take those steps, the problems would remain? Would it be worth your time? If you've already answered *"no,"* you can leave now, I thank you for playing. For those that said *"yes,"* I commend you on your choice.

Believe it or not, that one minute will be the most important minute of your whole day. That minute will be the seed you plant that is <u>guaranteed</u> to improve your life, slowly but surely. We all know that when we plant a seed, we do not get a crop overnight. Don't expect an overnight change here either. That will only discourage you and keep you from completing the process that is required to produce the results you desire.

What you do during that one minute is EXTREMELY IMPORTANT. You must fill your mind with information that will reprogram the part of you that is causing the problem, your subconscious mind. The stories in this book are designed to fit into your one-minute time slot. Each story is filled with practical information that provides answers to questions, solutions to problems and instructions for improvement that we all want and need. I know that most people will never read a whole book to find ways to improve their lives, so I've tried to summarize the most important parts of these books in each piece. And again, each story will take about one minute to read. Reading these daily messages will give your subconscious mind the information it needs to facilitate the change.

I ask you these questions: What if I'm wrong? What did it cost you? Only one minute each day. But what if I'm right and following the One-Minute Solution does improve your life? Imagine what your life would be like if you could improve

the areas you've always wanted to.
You now know how to proceed.
You now have the tools.
LET'S BEGIN NOW!

"Truth can only be found by seeking it."
- Plato

Open the Door

Many of us have a sincere desire to improve our lives. There are certain areas of our lives that are not at the level we'd like them to be, whether they have to do with relationships, health, or finances. In order to effectively improve those areas, we must first understand that we do not know everything and that the solutions to most of our problems lie in those areas that we may not yet know. We must be willing to venture into those unknown areas, no matter how painful they may appear. If not, the pain we are experiencing from our "problem areas" will eventually outweigh the temporary pain of the "solution areas."

It seems that our human nature, or ego, has a very hard time allowing in new information. It is very difficult and painful for our ego to admit that it may not know something. It has guarded our minds and put up a door that keeps most new information from entering. The solutions usually lie in the new information that is just waiting to be found and utilized.

But first, we must open the door and allow the solution to enter.

One of the most dangerous times on our path is when we think we know something. The moment we feel that way, we usually close the door to any new information because we think we already know it and nobody else can show us a better way.

Children grow so fast because they are aware that there are many things that they don't know and they have an intense desire to learn. When we become adults we figure we know it now and there is nothing left to learn. WRONG. As the famous college basketball coach John Wooden said, *"What you learn after you know everything is what really counts."* There is so much more to learn but it's not as easily recognized. We can always learn how to become better human beings, how to improve our lives and the lives of others, or how to solve problems that seem to keep repeating. In my opinion, there are no better things to learn.

In nature, it is said that if a plant is not growing, it's dying. When a potted plant outgrows its pot it must be placed in a bigger pot to accommodate the growth. It's the same with humans. We must constantly be trying to "expand our pots" of knowledge and, of course, put that knowledge into action or we will suffer the same consequence as the plant – a slow death. You can choose to live and grow and experience or you can choose to just bide time until it's time for you to "leave this place." The choice is yours.

So remember, the path of self-improvement can be sped up a great deal by following these points:
1. Admit that we don't know everything.
2. Seek the solution.
3. Open the door to allow the solution to enter.
4. Implement the solution.
5. Repeat Step 4 until the problem disappears.

"Your mind is like a parachute, it only works when it's open."
-Author Unknown

What Is "TRUE?"

Most people think that whatever they believe is *possible* is "TRUE" and what they consider to be *impossible* is "NOT TRUE." All you get from that point of view is your "version of the Truth." Most people's "version of the Truth" is what falls in between their belief paradigms, or boundaries. What is outside of those paradigms is considered "NOT TRUE." For example, 600 years ago people thought the Earth was flat. Their paradigms held this belief to be "TRUE," while the idea that the Earth was round fell outside of their paradigms and, therefore, was considered "NOT TRUE." In fact, if you would have tried to tell someone that the Earth was round, they would have thought you were crazy. Now, we all know that the Earth has always been round, but it wasn't until Columbus sailed the Atlantic, and proved this point, that people believed it to be "TRUE." What Columbus did was expand people's paradigm, so the idea that the Earth was round now fell within their boundaries and was considered "TRUE." The Earth did not change from flat to round, people's paradigm changed, meaning their "version of the Truth" changed. In other words, it doesn't really matter what you believe, certain things are "TRUE" regardless of what you think.

There are many TRUTHS in existence right now that fall outside of most people's paradigms, and considered "NOT TRUE." What you want to do is expand your paradigms to include these ideas into your belief structure. For example, there are many Universal Truths that people are not aware of, but would change their lives once they were understood. Many of the concepts I will be discussing may fall outside of your paradigms, but I ask that you keep an open mind as you read them. Whenever you read something that falls outside of your paradigm, and you believe to be "NOT TRUE," ask yourself *"Is it possible?"* You don't have to believe it immediately, just believe that it *might* be possible. When you do that, you are opening your mind to the possibility that it might exist. An open mind is the first step towards expanding your paradigms, which in turn, increases your awareness level and, therefore, dramatically improves your life.

> *"Some things are true, whether you believe in them or not."*
> -Nicholas Cage
> City of Angels

Universal Principles 101

#1 "There is no such thing as coincidence."
#2 "Everything happens for a reason."

Many people are aware of these two principles and, therefore, think they are armed with "spiritual armor" and ready to tackle the world's problems. Just knowing these two principles will not help improve your life until you understand the answer to the question that should be asked next. That question is:

"What is the reason?"

There is no simple answer to that question. I will try to provide answers in pieces throughout this book that individually can help improve lives and, collectively, can alter them dramatically.

> *"A coincidence is a small miracle in which God chooses to remain silent."*
> – Author Unknown

Do You Know How GREAT You Are?

No matter how strong our desire is to improve our lives, if we don't think we deserve success, it will not happen. Therefore, the most important part of this process is believing that we deserve all that we're capable of having.

While some of us may have been blessed with a family that praised us and helped us reach our potential, many people did not have the opportunity to receive such guidance. In fact, all that you heard were comments that put you down, told you how stupid you were and how you would never amount to anything. These words are for all of you who are resonating very strongly to what I just described and you know who you are.

If you ever heard words like that, you need to know they are NOT true. The only reason you heard those words is because the person telling you them (even if they were your loved ones) felt so bad about themselves that they needed to tell you those things to make themselves feel better. [Someone once said, "*There are two ways to have the tallest building, you*

can build it yourself or you can knock everyone else's down."]
Unfortunately, you heard them enough that you began to believe them. Since your beliefs create your reality, you started noticing that your reality was now proving what they were saying, thus reinforcing those FALSE beliefs.

The first thing you need to do is shed those FALSE beliefs and replace them with the RIGHT ones. The first one is, "*You are a magnificent human being capable of doing the extraordinary.*" Don't just take my word for it, look back at your life and you'll see that you have proved that statement to be true many times. Take a moment, right now, to think back to when you felt the most successful in your life. Maybe it was a time you aced an exam, or did something at work that you were praised for or even received an award. It could be as simple as creating a beautiful drawing, cooking a great meal, completing a difficult jigsaw or crossword puzzle, or obtaining your driver's license. I don't know the details of your life, but I'm sure that if you look back closely, you will realize that you've actually done some pretty amazing things. Spend some time everyday focusing on those past successes and feel how it feels to be successful. By doing this, you will attract more of the same into your life. You will shape your reality the way you want it to be.

The next one is, "*You deserve the life that you desire.*" If you knew your true essence, that you are spirit in human form, you'd realize how much you do deserve. Connect back with your Source and in time you will re-member everything you forgot.

From now on, let's not accept the old story, but instead create a new one. Remember, you're the main character and you control how it turns out.

"Our self image and our habits tend to go together. Change one and you will automatically change the other."
- Dr. Maxwell Maltz

A Gift from God

Imagine if God were to give you a gift. Do you think you'd enjoy the gift? Do you think it would be better than anything another person could give you? Of course it would be. God does not give questionable gifts. Now, do you think you could enjoy its benefits if you did not unwrap the gift and open the box? And what if there was some assembly required; would it be worth the effort? Certainly, after all, it's a gift from God. What could be better?

Well, God has given us all a gift. That gift is the benefits received when we apply His laws and teachings. But in order to receive the benefits, we must first "open the box" or read the books or material that contain these laws. There is "some assembly required," as we must apply what we read. Now if we complete these steps, we will receive the greatest gift we could imagine, as our lives will completely change and we will receive the gifts of *peace, love, health, happiness and abundance.*

> *"What you are is God's gift to you. What you make of yourself is your gift to God."*
> – Author Unknown

Rules for Being Human

- You will learn lessons.
- There are no mistakes – only lessons.
- A lesson is repeated until it is learned.
- If you don't learn easy lessons, they become harder.
(Pain is one way the universe gets your attention.)
- You will know you have learned a lesson when your
actions change.

Do you think you could play any game better if you understood the rules of that game? Well, in the "Game of Life," most people play without knowing the rules. That does not mean you're not subject to the penalties though. You see, whether you know the rules or not, they apply to everyone. You cannot call a "time-out." That being the case, I figured you might find these rules helpful while playing this "Game."

Once you realize that there are no mistakes, and that everything is just a lesson, you should not get upset when something doesn't go your way. Instead, ask yourself, *"What's the lesson here?"* Can you imagine how different your life would seem if you could always remember this? Do you realize that every time you got upset instead of figuring out the lesson, you only delayed the amount of time it took you to learn that lesson? I ask you, *"How long do you want to take to learn these lessons?"* You decide how fast or slow you go and it's usually determined by how much resistance you have to seeing the lesson. The more resistance you have, the more likely it is that pain will have to be used to get your attention. We all have a choice whether it's going to be an easy lesson or a painful one. For some reason, most of us choose the path of MOST resistance.

It doesn't have to be that way though. Understand that all of us have lessons that we need to learn. That's why we're here. The universe is always giving us real life scenarios to help us learn those lessons. If we don't learn the lesson, it will give us another similar scenario so we can make a new choice and demonstrate that we have learned the lesson. If we don't, the next scenario will be more difficult.

Be aware of the areas in your life that seem to have the most resistance (i.e. your financial situation – you're always broke; your personal relationships – every time you fall in love, the same thing happens; your health – you can never seem to get rid of that pain). That is life's way of telling you where the lesson is.

The first thing you need to do is identify the lesson, and then change your actions. If you can do this, you will enjoy this "Game" so much more.

"Know that everything in life has a purpose; there are no mistakes, no coincidences, all events are blessings given to us to learn from."
– Elisabeth Kubler-Ross

Less Resistance = More Speed

Those of you familiar with speed sports such as auto racing, skiing, bobsledding or swimming understand that each team or player wants to go as fast as possible and get to the finish line first. They all incorporate a little science into their sport to help them accomplish this goal. They understand that the less resistance they have, the faster they go. NASCAR's Jeff Gordon spends millions of dollars trying to lower his resistance and pick up that extra speed. That provides a very valuable lesson for everyday life. The less resistance we have to the challenges that life presents us, the faster we accomplish our goal. For us it's not so hard. All we have to do is change the way we look at the events (lessons) in our lives and make different choices and we will learn the lessons that much faster.

"What you resist, persists."
– Author Unknown

How Many Steps Will You Take?

The benefits of self-improvement – most of us want to experience them but so many of us are left wondering why we're not. We think we've done the work...we've read a few books...listened to a few tapes...said a few prayers...but we're not getting the results. Sometimes it gets so frustrating that we want to quit, thinking "that stuff doesn't work." Well, before we quit we should understand a few things first.

If we're not getting the results we want from doing "the work," it's not because IT doesn't work, but because *we're* not doing all we can. Even though we may have read a self-improvement book or two, most of us are not implementing the things we've learned. Experiencing the benefits of self-improvement does not happen just by reading a few books. It requires changing the many habits we've picked up throughout all the years of our lives. How foolish to think that it could all be changed by reading a few books. Certain books may trigger the desire to improve our lives, but the actual change will only occur after we've gone through the effort of changing our habits.

There's an old saying –*God says, 'Take one step towards Me, and I'll take one step towards you."* Notice who takes the first step. WE have to take the first step and then He will take one towards us and for every step we take, He also takes one. So I ask you, how many steps do you want God to take towards you? How much of God do you want to experience?

Too many of us want to experience all of the benefits without having to do any of the work. We want Him to take all of the steps towards us, without us taking any. Or, we take one and feel He should take all the rest. Sorry, the formula is "one for one." But one of His steps is a lot greater than one of ours. Believe me; it's worth every bit of effort to receive the benefits that await all of us.

If you are willing to take the necessary steps, here are a few I recommend:

1. Decide that you really want to improve your life and are willing to do what it takes. (You can either do this now or wait until the universe is forcing you to do this by bringing pain or crisis into your life.)
2. Look at yourself honestly and decide what areas you need to work on.
3. Seek out the tools that will help transform your life (books, tapes, seminars, etc.).
4. APPLY WHAT YOU LEARN!!!!
5. Keep doing this until you are reaping the rewards of your efforts.

Once you realize that you are creating the things that show up in your life, either deliberately or by default, you will want to take control of the process and start taking the steps that will create the masterpiece that you're capable of.

"God gives food to every bird, but he does not throw it into the nest."
- Montenegrin proverb

How to Change a Habit

In order to improve your life, you are going to have to change some of your bad habits. The first thing you want to do is identify the action you want to change. In order for a habit to change, it has to go through four phases. First, you are what I call *"Unconsciously Incompetent"* which means you are doing that action without being aware of it. You must become aware whenever you are doing that action, which is called *"Consciously Incompetent."* You do not have to change it yet, just be aware that you are doing it and that you need to change it. Every time you realize that you have to change that action, you are one step closer to a permanent change. Eventually, you will become *"Consciously Competent"* which means that you will have to *try* to choose the new action you would like to demonstrate. This will take time and effort, so don't get discouraged. It is said that something becomes a habit after being repeated 100 times. Finally, you will become *"Unconsciously Competent"* which means that you are choosing the new action without even thinking about it.

Changing a habit is like getting in shape. If you want to have lasting results that you can see and feel, you don't go to the gym once and become *"in-shape."* It is a process and requires repetition. It's the same when changing a habit; it's a process and requires repetition.

In order to change some of the more difficult habits to break, the ones that are not easily identified, I recommend a few things. First, feed yourself with information that can help improve your life, such as a self-help or inspirational book like this one. You will not learn anything to the degree necessary to change a habit just by reading it once because you are only learning it on a surface level. You must read it many times, until it gets into your subconscious mind. For example, read some of the stories in this book 10 times. Each time you read it, it will become ingrained on a deeper and more permanent level. Next, become aware. Life has a way of giving you a real life example to practice what you are trying to learn. Learning something in theory means nothing. Being able to apply and demonstrate what you have learned is what counts. (Ask anybody that has gone to medical school.) You will be given many chances to apply what you've learned and change your habit. Do not try to change many habits at one time. This will only discourage you. Choose one, master it, then choose another. As time goes on, this process will become easier. Ask yourself *"Do you want to be the master of your actions, or do you want your actions to master you?"*

"As with the creation of a diamond from coal, the transformation in the human being usually requires sufficient time and sufficient pressure."
- Robin Norwood

Re-act or New-act?

We all know what the word "REACT" means. We see that re-act means to act as we've acted before. Think about all the times that you are forced to react. Sometimes your reaction is appropriate, but sometimes your choice may not serve you. What you want to do at those times is choose a new way to act or "NEW-ACT." How do we get to the point where we choose to "new-act" instead of "re-act?" First, let's try to understand how our brain works.

Our brain is like a filing cabinet, which stores whatever information is put into it. There are only two ways information gets into this "filing cabinet," through our own experiences and from the experiences of others that we have been exposed to. When we are in a situation that requires us to choose a response, our brain searches its files for a similar circumstance and chooses the appropriate "file" or response. All of this occurs in a matter of milliseconds. As you can see, we are obviously limited by the types of "files" that are stored in our brain. Our solution is to change the "files" by adding more beneficial "files" or responses to our "cabinet." We don't have too much control over the circumstances that we experience, but we can control the types of experiences of others that we allow ourselves to store. We should expose ourselves to the experiences of people who demonstrate the types of choices we would like to make. What I've found works best for me is to seek out the qualities in certain people that I'd like to emulate. I choose people that demonstrate to the highest order such as Jesus, Buddha, Gandhi, Mother Theresa, etc. They are wonderful teachers for all of us. The greatest lessons they taught us were by example. The way they lived their lives was the way they demonstrated what they taught. When I am confronted with a choice, I ask myself, *"What would Jesus (or Buddha, etc.) do now?"* If someone steals something from me, or cuts me off in traffic, or says something I don't like, or does something that harms me, and I have the choice to re-act, I immediately ask myself that question. My brain now has another "file" it can access and presents me with another choice, and I "new-act" instead of "re-act."

The world we live in is built by the choices we make. Now we are aware of how those choices are made. Let's all commit to making new choices, or "new-acting" and we will all contribute to the creation of a place where we want our children to grow up, a place called "Heaven on Earth." It is our destiny. We hold the key.

"The definition of Insanity is doing the same thing over and over again and expecting different results."
- Author Unknown

How to Find the "Treasure"

We've all seen the movies involving a search for hidden treasures. The lead character has a map and has to find the clues to reach the treasure. The clues are not obvious when looked at on the surface but after looking a little deeper, or shifting one's focus, they become clear.

An example most people can relate to are those paintings in the mall that look like beautiful graphic pictures on the surface, but reveal a hidden, 3-D image when you've shifted your focus. Not everybody can see the 3-D image. I've seen people look at those pictures for 20 minutes, trying hard to locate what seems to be hidden. The harder they try, the less likely it is that they will ever see the image. The way to shift your focus is to relax and not try too hard, and your focus seems to shift automatically.

We are all searching for a "hidden treasure" in life although some people are not even aware of it. We are all searching for INNER PEACE. We think we can attain it by reaching certain goals or acquiring certain objects. Most people feel that if they just had enough money, or the right position with the right company, or if they were married (or single again), or were happier with their appearance, or had the new house or car, they could reach that level of inner peace they so desire. Most of the times when they reach that goal, they find there is still something missing, so they find something else that they think will do it. I call it the unquenchable thirst. No matter how many of their goals they reach, they still feel unfulfilled. The reason is because they are EGO goals. Satisfying an ego desire will not bring about the level of inner peace that one is capable of reaching. That can only be done by satisfying the goals of your INNER SPIRIT.

How do we find out how to satisfy our inner spirit? By shifting our focus so we can see the clues that our spirit is leaving for us. Most people do not realize it but our spirit is trying to lead us to a state of inner peace. This path usually has many detours (called life's lessons) that seem to make it a bit bumpy. It doesn't have to be so bumpy, though. When we become aware of the signs, or clues that are all around us, it's as if our spirits are paving the path in front of us. It is not something that can be figured out by the brain, because the brain is the vehicle that your ego uses to interpret information and make decisions. Your spirit uses something much deeper, your sixth sense, which is a feeling you can learn to develop the more you get in touch with your inner spirit.

Once we learn how to shift from the vision of ego to the vision of spirit, the clues to the "treasure" will become clear.

"We can choose to see life as a series of trials and tribulations, or we can choose to see life as an accumulation of treasures."
– Author Unknown

Hidden Treasures

*Gold…Diamonds…Oil…*Three of the most valuable commodities produced by the Earth. Where are they found? Hidden deep beneath the surface of the Earth.

God has provided us with monetary treasures and has placed them well beneath the surface, knowing that not everyone can reach them. But when they are found, they can dramatically improve lives.

He has done the same thing with His spiritual treasures. You may read the Bible, or the Koran, or any other divinely inspired work, and you may only receive what is on the surface. Hidden deep beneath the surface are the REAL treasures, the ones that can dramatically improve lives.

Let's not be satisfied with the meaning that we see on the surface. Let's dig a little deeper so we can enjoy the "riches" of the most valuable treasures given to man.

"In your exploration of Truth, see to it that you do not rest satisfied in the yellow (surface) clay of a few spiritual discoveries, but press on to the rich blue clay underneath."
– Emmet Fox

Follow the "Signs"

We are all on an eternal journey of spiritual evolution. These bodies; this time in history; and the circumstances we find ourselves in at this time, were all chosen by our spirits for our optimum growth. Every "spirit in human form" has a great mission that they chose to undertake here on Earth. They all differ in details but remain the same in their overall goal – Spiritual Evolution. One of the requirements of our mission is that we "forget" what we know as spirits. We are forced to navigate through the challenges that are presented to us in order to initiate the growth process. Many years ago, when people first started navigating the planet, by land or sea, they were led by the signs that God left for them, the stars. They knew that no matter how far off course they were, no matter what their brains may have told them, or how they felt at the time, they were assured that God's signs would ALWAYS lead the way.

God has left signs for our spiritual journey, as well. Those signs are the SPIRITUAL TRUTHS that have been around for thousands of years. Our spirits knew before they got here that when they were lost, they could always look for those signs to help them find their way. The only way to truly understand the deepest meaning of even the most simple signs is to look at them through the eyes of spirit, not the eyes we've grown accustomed to using, the eyes of ego. When looked at properly, everything becomes clear.

When confronted with our everyday challenges, the first thing we have to be aware of is where the resistance is coming from. That is where the lesson is; that is where we are being forced to grow. If we sense resistance coming from another person or circumstance, we are being forced to look at ourselves and figure out what we need to learn about OURSELVES (such as demonstrating love, compassion, non-judgment, patience, forgiveness, etc.). Then, we have to see how to handle the lesson using the proper spiritual truths (signs from God). Remember, no matter how lost we may be, how we may feel at the time or how our brains may tell us to solve the problem, the answer ALWAYS lies in the spiritual truths. Any other answer keeps us in the lesson and keeps the resistance or pain in our lives.

Many people know these Truths in theory; the universe requires that we demonstrate what we know. In order for our "missions" to continue, we must demonstrate these Truths. Only then can we proceed. Remember, it's not a question of "If" but "When." We provide the answer.

"Perceive that which cannot be seen with the eye."
– Musahi Miyamoto

How to "Melt the Ice"

If you want to melt an ice cube, all you have to do is place it near a heat source. The ice does not have to do anything; it does not have to *try* to melt. As long as it's near the heat source, everything happens automatically.

One of the keys to unlocking our spiritual understanding, or "melting our ice" is demonstrated very simply by that example. As long as we are exposed to our "heat source," or spiritual truths, we will eventually begin to understand higher truths, and see the bigger picture. That is when the struggle subsides and life begins to flow with effortless ease.

Many people read spiritual works, and think they've learned what they need to know, but their lives don't improve, or "the ice does not melt." Reading something once or twice is never enough to "melt the ice." You must read the spiritual works many times, knowing that as long as you are exposing yourself to the "Source," you are slowly, but surely, "melting the ice."

This probably seems "too good to be true" but it can be just that simple. A wise man once said, *"For a small reward a man will hurry away on a long journey, while for eternal life many will hardly take a single step."* Unfortunately most people will not put in that extra effort required to eventually live a life which does not require so much effort.

"He who cannot change the very fabric of his thought will never be able to change reality, and will never, therefore, make any progress."
– Anwar Sadat

Knowledge Is Nothing – Demonstration Is Everything

Many people have heard the term "Knowledge Is Power." That is not a complete statement. "*Applied* Knowledge is Power" is more accurate. Knowledge means nothing if it is not applied to everyday life. The world is full of people who possess a tremendous amount of knowledge but are unable to demonstrate any of it. How many lawyers or policemen do we know that break the law? How many doctors do not follow their own advice? How many priests truly follow what they teach about the Bible? All of these men have a great deal of knowledge about the professions they are in, but obviously it does not stop there. In order to truly make a difference in this world, we must *apply* and *demonstrate* what we learn. Only then, will we see the results in a positive way on a worldwide scale.

For most people, it's the same thing with understanding spiritual principles. There are so many people who have read books, gone to seminars, listened to tapes, meditated for hours, but are still unable to demonstrate the simplest universal principles. The reason why we study and learn something is so that we can be prepared the next time life offers us an opportunity to demonstrate what we've learned. When we leave this place called "Earth," and move to the next part of our journey, we will find that there was no point system awarded for how much knowledge we possessed, how many facts we had stored in our brains. The only thing that will matter will be how many times we demonstrated spiritual principles such as love, forgiveness, acceptance, non-judgment, patience, giving and compassion. How many times have we seen people come out of church on Sunday morning and immediately start gossiping about people? How many times have we cursed someone out for cutting us off while driving? How many times have we gotten angry at our spouse or children and taken out our anger on them? How many times have we looked at someone and noticed and judged their differences instead of understanding that they are people just like us? It is precisely in those moments that we are required to demonstrate a spiritual principle.

We are all responsible for how we choose to act in every moment. Our world is built by those moments. If we all choose a new way to act, abiding by spiritual principles, we will all play a big part in changing the world, moment by moment, action by action, choice by choice.

Be aware of the choices you make from now on, and ask yourself, *"What kind of world am I helping to build?"*

"The longest part of the spiritual journey is from the head to the heart."
- Andrew Moss

The Movie Called "Your Life"

Did you realize that you are the director and main character of a great movie called *"Your Life?"* Let's review how it works.

When you watch a movie in the theater, you are watching everything take place on the giant screen. It all starts with a roll of film. The film is put through the projector where the light goes through the film, projecting it onto the big screen. If you don't like what you are seeing on the screen, do you try to change what's on the screen? Of course not, you know that would never work. In order to change what's on the screen, you must change the film that's in the projector.

The movie called *"Your Life"* works the same way. The giant screen is your reality. The film is your consciousness, or the thoughts that are running through your mind at EVERY moment. The vibration, or energy your body gives off is the light that comes through the projector. Now if you want to change what's on the giant screen of your life, or your everyday REALITY, do you try to keep changing the outside circumstances (the screen) or do you think you might be more successful if you simply changed your consciousness (the film)? Most people are unaware of this. That is why they always try to change their lives by changing their outer circumstances. Changing an outer circumstance without changing your consciousness can not improve the situation. In other words, for anything to change in your "outer" world, you must first change your "inner" world.

How do you go about changing the "film," or your consciousness? First, and most important, is you have to be aware of the type of "film" you have put into your "projector." In other words, you must be aware of your thoughts at EVERY moment. Most people say that their thoughts are fine and that there is nothing to change. Well that is guaranteed to keep you in the same "scene." Be aware of every time you have a negative thought, such as anger, fear, worry, impatience, judgment, or jealousy. Those thoughts are projected into your reality and show up as what we call "problems." You want to replace them with thoughts of love, faith, patience, non-judgment and acceptance. You have spent your whole life to this point, choosing the same type of "film," so changing your thoughts will not happen overnight. It is a process that will require time, effort and patience. Not changing the "film" will require greater effort and more patience. Think about the way the rest of this movie called *"Your Life"* could turn out now that you understand how to change it. Let's all be an Oscar winning director and create the best "movie" possible.

"The world is what we think it is. If we can change our thoughts, we can change the world."
– H. M. Tomlinson

Rise Above Your Problems

Everybody's lives are filled with opportunities to grow that come disguised as daily challenges. The mistake most people make is that they consider these challenges to be "problems." Then what they do is focus on the problem, which gives it energy, as fuel does to a fire. As long as you give "fuel" to the problem, it will remain in your life. In order to learn the lesson that is being presented, you must first rise above the problem, where your vision will be clear enough to learn the lesson.

Nature provides us with a wonderful example. If you've ever watched a cat with a puppy that wants to play, you will see that it will put up with it for a while, then it will hiss at the puppy and maybe even take a swipe at it. After a while it realizes it has a choice, it can remain in the turmoil that the puppy is creating or it can rise above it. The cat will usually jump up on to a table or somewhere that is not accessible to the puppy. You will then notice the cat relax and start cleaning himself, which shows that the cat is truly in the present moment and not thinking about how annoying that puppy was. In other words, the problem does not exist anymore. We can all learn a lot from animals. They all live in the present moment and do not hold on to things from the past, like humans do.

The first key is to understand that the "problem" is actually an opportunity to grow. That will allow you to look at what's happening with a different mind frame. Then, you must remember to remain in the present moment, which means to forget about, or let go of the past. Challenges can only be solved in the present moment if our minds and our vision are clear. Most people are walking around today holding on to thoughts about things that did not go their way in the past. It's like garbage in the basement. Everybody has too much of it and most, if not all of it, is useless.

If you focus on the problem, you will remain in the problem. If you focus on the solution, it will always present itself. Once again, we see that whatever we focus on creates our reality. So in order to change our reality, we MUST change what we are focusing on. A wise man once said, *"I cannot control what people say or do, I can only control how I feel about what people say or do."* If you understand that to its deepest level, it will bring a freedom that you cannot imagine. Do that and watch your "problems" fly away.

"Reflect upon your present blessings, of which every man has many; not on your past misfortunes, of which all men have some."
– Charles Dickens

Rise Above Your Problems—Part 2

If you've ever flown in a plane, I'm sure you can remember a time that the plane hit some turbulence. Some people are mildly annoyed by it; some people get nauseous, while others fear for their lives. What is the solution to this problem? Very simple. All the pilot does is take the airplane to a higher altitude and rise above the turbulence. Pilots know that if they fly at a certain altitude, they will fly over most of the turbulence, or "problems."

Let that be an example in your life. Do NOT remain in the turbulence of your life, seek to find the solution and it will be smooth skies ahead.

Once again, we are presented with an answer to one of life's many challenges. Life always presents solutions to our challenges. If we can become a student of life, we will keep graduating to higher levels of understanding. To those that do, go the "diplomas" or rewards of inner peace.

"Everyone and everything around you is your teacher."
- Ken Keyes, Jr.

Sail Through the Storm

Sometimes life seems to get too difficult to handle. You are in a point of extreme pain and the solution is nowhere in sight. I call that one of the *"Storms of Life."* How do we navigate to safety when we are struggling with one of those violent storms? How does the captain of a ship navigate through a storm at sea?

The most important thing is to be prepared. The captain will have information about the storm, he will know exactly how to steer his vessel and he will keep his composure throughout. In order to get through your "storm," you must do the same.

First, you must have information on your "storm," in other words, why are you in the situation you are in? The more you know about why you're in the situation, the easier it will be to get out of. Hidden in the reason is every solution.

Next, you must know exactly how to steer your "vessel," or you must understand how your life really works. Most people lead their lives like a ship without a rudder. They have no idea why things happen to them and they find themselves lost or not headed in the direction they thought they were going. When you understand how your life works, or how the choices you make and the thoughts you think actually create your everyday reality, you can get yourself back on course. Do everything you can to understand how everything in life REALLY works. (Hint: It's not taught in schools.) Just as the captain of a ship requires a great deal of training to navigate a ship, human beings require training to "navigate their own vessels" through life's journey.

Finally, you must keep your composure throughout the storm. You can get through every tough challenge in life when you keep cool and stay in the proper mind frame required to find a solution. The captain knows that behind every storm is a clear sky, and just behind every problem in your life lies a solution. The "storms" in your life are always temporary, although they may seem like they're going to last forever when you're going through them. Just knowing this will allow you to relax and say, *This too shall pass."*

Next time you find yourself going through one of those "storms," know that you have what it takes to sail through to safety.

"God sometimes takes us into troubled waters, not to drown us,
but to cleanse us."
– Author Unknown

School of Life

When you were in school, you were always given tough lessons to learn, tested on those lessons, given a summer break, and then headed back for the next grade. Your life works the same way. Most people tend to think that when they finished school, they were through learning. Actually, school just taught you *how* to learn, so you could be prepared to get through the *"School of Life."* The entrance exam is "being born" and it usually starts when we are around 18 – 21. The lessons of life are not optional; they are all required learning. You go through a challenge in life, you are tested on what you've learned to see if you can apply it, you are given a break, and then the next lesson of life begins. It's important to understand this because some people may wonder why life never seems to get easy, it always seems like the struggle never ends. If you look at life as a school that we are all enrolled in, it removes the struggle because you know you are exactly where you're supposed to be.

Make sure you learn what you're here to learn so you can graduate to the next level. You wouldn't want to get left back, would you?

"Difficulties mastered are opportunities won."
– Sir Winston Churchill

This Is Only a "Test"

Remember when you were in school and you had a fire drill. You knew it was a drill or a "test," so you remained calm and left the building in an orderly manner. If the fire alarm went off unexpectedly, everybody would panic, your heart would be racing and there would be a great deal of confusion.

In life, it's the same thing. Understand that in your moment of panic, hardship or resistance, you are in the "heart" of the test. Say to yourself, *"This is only a test. If this had been an actual emergency..."* You will become detached from the situation and be able to observe it objectively. You will immediately relax and be in a better position to solve the problem and get out of the uncomfortable or painful situation.

Remember, your life is a series of tests, and once you realize it, you can become the master of your own circumstances.

"Good people are good because they've come to wisdom through failure. We get very little wisdom from success, you know."
-William Saroyan

Accept Responsibility

Would you believe me if I told you there is no such thing as a *"victim?"* "Victim" is the word used to describe people who find themselves in situations where they feel they've been wronged or harmed. In reality, that does not exist. When we become aware that there is a deeper meaning behind everything, we come to see that every event is connected in some way to other events that preceded it. Just because we are not aware of the connection, does not mean that it does not exist. Just because I cannot see the air I breathe, does not mean that it does not exist. When we are not aware of the connections, we call ourselves *"victims."*

First, we must understand that we create (which means we are RESPONSIBLE for) EVERYTHING that happens in our lives. Remember, every situation we go through in life is designed to teach us something. We may think we have mastered certain lessons but understand, we do not grade our own work. The universe does, and only IT knows what areas we still need to work on. Therefore, certain situations will continuously be created until we can demonstrate to the universe that we have truly learned the lesson by making the "highest" choice at that moment.

We must realize then, that we *attract* the situations in our lives that can help us accomplish this. Once this is understood, we can see <u>how</u> we are responsible for everything in our lives.

Accepting responsibility is one of the most important things you can do to change your life. It is extremely empowering. *Empower* means to give power or energy to something. When you accept responsibility, you empower yourself and give yourself the energy that is required to change and improve your life. When you deny responsibility and put the blame or responsibility for the "problems" in your life onto outside circumstances or other people, you are depleting or giving away your energy. You are putting energy into the things and events outside of you. Improving your life requires energy, and it can <u>not</u> happen if you keep giving your energy away. In other words, if you just got into an argument with your spouse, or you just got fired from your job, or you had something stolen from you (yes, that's right, you are responsible for the events that transpired that created the scenario that something was stolen from you), it is NEVER 100% the other person's fault.

First, accept responsibility for the situation you are in. Then, ask yourself these questions:

1. What did I do to contribute to this circumstance?
2. What could I do now to rectify this situation?
3. What could I do from now on to avoid being in this situation again?

Those are questions that will *always* provide a solution. And now that you have retained your own energy, you will have the power to create the improvement you desire.

"People generally think that it is the world, the environment, external relationships, which stand in one's way, in the way of one's good fortune…and at the bottom it is always man himself that stands in his own way."
-Kierkegaard

Your Dream Garden

Most people have dreams they'd like to see come true. There is a way to make that happen; you just have to know how to do it, or cultivate what I call your *"Dream Garden."*

In order to produce a beautiful flower garden, you must first plant the seeds. Then, do what you can to help the flowers grow such as fertilize the soil and water the seeds. You must also pull the weeds that can destroy the flowers you hope to grow. The rest must be left up to nature, which is to provide the necessary sunlight and time to allow the flowers to develop. It is very important that you do not interfere with nature's process. The final step is to have faith that the flowers will grow; in other words, do not keep digging up the seeds to see if they are growing. Know that in time a beautiful flower will emerge from that tiny seed.

Just as every flower starts as a seed, every dream starts as a thought. You must carefully choose the thought you would like to see "blossom" into reality. Once the "seed" is planted, you must do your work. Just as the fertile soil and water you give the seed helps it grow, you must nourish the thought if you'd like it to come true. The feelings behind the thought provide the nourishment that is required for your dream to become a reality. The thought should bring about a positive feeling in you (how you would feel if you had what you desire), not a negative feeling, such as need (you *must* have it) or lack (I feel broke or empty without it). Negative feelings will keep your desire from reaching you. They will repel the positive feelings you would like to have if your desire became real. Nourishing the thought with positive feelings attracts your desired outcome until it shows up in your life. Be careful not to include any negative thoughts like, *"This will never work,"* or *"I still don't see it yet, it's not going to show up,"* as those are the weeds that will strangle the beautiful "flower" (desire) you're trying to grow.

Next, you must allow nature to do its part, meaning you must allow the Universal Laws to take over. When you understand the Law of Attraction, you realize that like attracts like kind, and in time, the thought you have planted will eventually show up, if you have nourished it with a positive feeling. Now you must wait and allow it to show up. The last step is to have faith and KNOW that it will appear. You don't want to keep wondering everyday why it hasn't shown up yet or when it's going to happen. That would be the same as uncovering the seed and checking to see if it's growing. KNOW that when the time is right, your dream will become a reality.

I recommend spending five minutes each day tending to your *"Dream Garden."* Believe it or not, there is nothing you can do on an outer level that is more effective. You need to be aware that you are attracting the things that are already happening in your life. This process will help you improve the quality of what shows up. From now on, try to grow the most beautiful bed of "flowers" in your "garden."

"A man sooner or later discovers that he is the master gardener of his soul, the director of his life."
- James Allen

Live or Exist

What is it that we are all REALLY trying to do in life? Our
main goal is to create a state of peace and joy in our lives.
What creates a feeling of joy in us? It could be spending time
with our loved ones, playing with our children, spending time
in nature, helping those in need, or simply creating, whether
it be through music, art, cooking, etc. Everyone knows what
creates that feeling in their own life. It amazes me how much
of our time we are willing to trade doing something that we
may not enjoy in order to achieve that state of peaceful being.
We work at jobs or careers that we may not be happy in so
we can have enough money to do the things we think will
bring us that joy. We are willing to give away most of our
waking hours in order to experience that joy for a few hours
on the weekend or when we retire. Unfortunately, we find
out after we retire that we did not accomplish what we hoped
we would and come to realize the time we traded is lost and
we cannot get it back.

Let's examine why we work so hard and strive for more money, a bigger house, a new car or whatever material object it may be. We think that having that object will make us feel better. In other words, we are really trying to make ourselves *feel better*. We all think that feeling better comes from something in our outer world. That's why we are all searching for "outer" things to help us attain that state of joy and peace. Acquiring things on an "outer" level can help us feel better, but only temporarily. Feeling better *permanently* only happens when we attain that feeling on an "inner" level.

Some of us are blessed enough to have found out what it is that brings us joy and earn a living, even a substantial one, while doing it. When you do that you are *"living."* When you can't do that and have to work (I define "work" as trading your time for money), you are *"existing."* A good barometer to gauge if you are *"living"* or *"existing"* is to ask yourself this question: If I did not get paid for what I'm doing, would I still do it? If the answer is no, don't quit your job today. Just promise yourself that you will find what it is you would love to do, even if you didn't get paid. In time, the opportunity will present itself to allow you to do what your heart desires and get paid for doing it. The choice is yours – do you want to *"live"* and create an experience of peace and joy or do you want to *"exist"* and just get through each day?

"If you choose a job that you like you will never have to work a day in your life."
- Confucius

Live or Evil

Whether we want to believe it or not, we create everything that happens in our lives, both good and bad. Just as the Law of Gravity is always at work, so too are Universal Laws. When we allow Universal Laws to work *for us* instead of *against us*, we create circumstances that we consider to be *"good."* Ignorance of the laws does not matter; every one of us is subject to them at all times.

When we are living in accordance with Universal Laws, we create a state of harmony in our lives. When we do not live in accordance to Universal Laws, we create a life that is out of harmony or balance and filled with chaos.

"Live" spelled backwards is *"evil."* When our lives are headed in the wrong direction, things that we consider "bad" or "evil" will appear in our lives. We must realize that the direction in which we are headed, or the choices we make and the thoughts we think, will determine the quality of the events that show up in our lives. Sometimes we must stop

and reflect on the direction we are headed in and make the necessary adjustments that will allow us to reach our destination. In this case our destination is *"Inner Peace."*

"Whatever good you have is all from God. Whatever evil, all is from yourself."
- The Koran

Everlasting Life

Many people believe *"everlasting life"* is a condition that can be attained IF we believe, follow or do certain things. It is actually a condition that EXISTS now and forever. As the name implies, *"everlasting life"* lasts forever. It has no end AND it has no beginning. In other words, your life did not start when you were born and it will not end when you die. Your life has been in existence since "forever" before you were born and will continue to exist "forever" after you die. The words "born" and "die" only represent what happens to your physical body. Understand that you are much more than your physical body. Your TRUE form is that of spirit, the part of you that exists forever. The body is just the vehicle your spirit utilizes to navigate through this temporary journey.

You may own a car to help you get through life but you are not nor will you ever be mistaken for that car. When you no longer have use for that particular car, you will get rid of it. It is the same with your physical "vehicle," or body. The physical body allows you to experience life here in the physical world that your spirit could not experience otherwise. When your spirit has no more use for the body, it discards it (what you call "die").

We all have become so attached to life in the physical world that we do not see the bigger picture. We believe that all we have is this limited time in our bodies and then comes – *The Great Unknown*. Sometimes, the fear of *"The Unknown"* is so great that it affects the time we spend here. We fear our own deaths, we fear or worry about the deaths of our loved ones and then mourn them when they are gone. We spend so much time attaching a negative emotion to the concept of "death" that it affects our ability to LIVE. All because we do not understand the bigger picture. When you can see the bigger picture, everything seems much smaller.

A great book is made up of great chapters, which in turn are made up of great pages. Think of your life as only one chapter in a great book instead of the book itself. Each day represents one page in that chapter. Every day of your life you write a new page in the chapter called *"Who I Am Now."* Your goal is to make each page in this chapter of the great book called *"Your Everlasting Life"* as beautiful as you can. The wonderful thing is that even though each person's chapter may end differently, everyone's book has the same ending...EVERLASTING LIFE.

"We are not human beings having a spiritual experience. We are spiritual beings having a human experience."
- Pierre Teilhard de Chardin

You're More Attractive Than You Think

Everyone is always trying to make themselves more attractive. Unfortunately, they usually try to fix their "outer shell." The word *"attract"* means "to pull things towards you." Well, I have news for you. You are more attractive than you think. You are constantly attracting the things, events and people that show up in your life and you're not even aware of it. All of the "GOOD" things and all of the "BAD" things that show up are attracted by you. You are probably wondering how that's possible. It's actually very simple when you understand how the *Law of Attraction* works. This is one of the Universal Laws that are ALWAYS in effect whether you are aware of them or not, and whether you believe in them or not. Do you think someone who fell off of a cliff 5,000 years ago did not get hurt or die? I'm sure he did not know what the Law of Gravity was but you can be sure it was still in effect.

The Law of Attraction states, *"that which is like itself is drawn to itself."* Our main points of attraction are our thoughts and feelings. Simply stated, the thoughts you think and the feelings you feel are attracting EVERYTHING into your reality. Let's try to put this in a way that is easy to understand. We all have things that we desire and things that we do not desire. When you are feeling *positive* feelings, you are attracting what you *desire*. Positive feelings include love, joy, laughter, peace, patience, acceptance and faith. When you are feeling *negative* feelings, you are attracting the things you *do not desire* and pushing away the things that you desire. Negative feelings include anger, fear, worry, jealousy, greed, impatience and judgment. The stronger your *feeling*, the stronger your attraction is, or the faster you are pulling something towards you.

Your power to create lies in the way you FEEL. The most important thing you could do to improve your life is to CHANGE THE WAY YOU FEEL. Most people never monitor how they feel. They complain about their problems and the problems of society to anyone who will listen or they allow others to complain to them. They gossip to their friends about everyone, bringing up all the things that bother them. They watch the news on TV, which is mostly negative, and then wonder why they feel so bad. All the while, they are attracting things they *do not desire*. I'm sure if most people where aware of what they were actually doing to themselves, they would stop doing it. Remember, there are things that are going on behind the surface that helps everything make sense. Most people are not aware of them because we were never taught them. That doesn't mean they don't exist. Learn them, understand them, apply them and change your life.

"There is a basic law that like attracts like. Negative thinking definitely attracts negative results. Conversely, if a person habitually thinks optimistically and hopefully, his positive thinking sets in motion creative forces and success, instead of eluding him, flows toward him."
– Norman Vincent Peale

Your Ship of Desires

Let's say there are two ships in the water. One is called "*Things I Desire*" and it contains everything you want. The other is called "*What I Do NOT Desire*" and contains everything you don't want. In order to pull the boats to you, you must pull on a rope that is attached to them. Which boat would you choose? Easy choice, right?

Well, the principles of life work the same way; only there is no rope. Instead of pulling our ships towards us with a rope, we pull them towards us with our FEELINGS. Every time we are feeling GOOD, we are pulling the rope to the ship called "*Things I Desire*" and every time we are feeling BAD, we are pulling in the ship called "*What I Do NOT Desire*" and pushing away "*Things I Desire.*" The stronger we FEEL, either GOOD or BAD, the faster we are "pulling on the rope." Which boat are you pulling in everyday? Now that you are aware of how it works, be careful of which "rope" you're pulling on. When you find yourself pulling in the wrong boat, change the way you feel and you will change the boat you are pulling towards you.

"Faith is an invisible and invincible magnet, and attracts to itself whatever it fervently desires and calmly and persistently expects."
– Ralph W. Trine

The Ruler of the Castle

In order to improve our lives, it would be best if we better understood ourselves. Most people have become attached to the idea that they are their physical bodies. You must realize that life in this physical body is only temporary. Your life is eternal, but in the form of spirit. Your spirit is the energy that gives life to your body. As human beings, we tend to forget our spiritual nature and rely solely on what our brain tells us.

When a baby is born, it is a spirit with a new body form. It is lost in a new world, but still carries some of the characteristics of the spirit, namely *unconditional love.* The baby's mother provides a safe space for the baby by returning that unconditional love. One day, the mother gets upset at the baby and its whole world changes. It realizes for the first time that love is conditional. That is a very scary moment for the baby and that is when the ego starts developing. The ego is created to protect us through this difficult journey. EGO can stand for *Earth Guide Only*. As time goes on, the ego develops further and starts making most of our decisions. Our spirit takes a back seat to the dominant ego, sitting quietly awaiting a reason that it will be called back into action.

An analogy I like to use is that of a ruler in a castle. The castle is run by someone who sees all as equal, realizes everyone is on the same side, knows there is nothing to fear and rules with the power of Love. The permanent ruler has temporarily allowed a new ruler to inhabit the castle. This ruler sees everyone as a threat to its power and lives in fear of its enemies, as well as the rightful ruler of the castle. It feels its value is based on accumulating power and material possessions.

Human beings have allowed a temporary ruler (ego) to inhabit their castle, but in time, the permanent ruler (spirit) will reclaim his throne. The ego is full of fear because it knows it's only "renting the castle" it resides in and it's just a matter of time before the rightful owner comes back and takes over. What we would like to do is get in touch with our spirit and allow it to guide our decisions and actions. When you are confronted with a choice to make, try to figure out what is motivating your decision. Is it motivated by fear, anger, jealousy, revenge, scarcity or lack, winning at all costs, giving somebody what they deserve or "it helps me today and I don't care about tomorrow"? If it is, then it is motivated by ego. You want to ask what your spirit would do in that situation. It will always lead you in a better direction and that is towards peace for all involved.

Your ego thinks this life is the whole puzzle, your spirit *knows* this is just a small piece of a larger puzzle. Follow your spirit and behold the masterpiece you can create.

"The great truth is that man is a spiritual being, who brings with him a life to unfold, a power to release, a love to express, and a veritable kingdom of heaven to outpicture. He doesn't begin life empty, but as a dynamic spiritual potentiality."
- Eric Butterworth

Your Inner Guide

If you were going on a trip to a foreign land, do you think having a guide with you might make getting around a little easier? Do you think you could get to a specific destination more quickly if you followed the guide's instructions instead of trying to figure it out yourself? Of course you would.

On this journey we are all on called *"Life,"* we come here like visitors in a foreign land. The good news is we are ALL provided with a guide to help us get around a little easier and reach our destination. Our spirit is our *"Inner Guide"* and it communicates to us all the time as it tries to direct us in our lives. Most people are not aware of this guidance and, therefore, are not able to understand it when it's given. Our spirit exists in a state of peace and harmony and knows that this is our natural state. Its desire for us is to remain in that state and it will try to guide us in a direction where we can attain it.

Our *Inner Guide* communicates to us through our *FEELINGS*. When we are doing or thinking about something that is leading us towards peace, it will give us a GOOD feeling, which means it wants us to proceed in that direction. An example that most people can relate to is when you get goose bumps. Usually, you get goose bumps when something touches you deeply. That is your spirit communicating to you very strongly because you have touched it and it is touching you back. When we are doing or thinking about something that is leading us away from peace, it will give us a BAD feeling, which is telling us to change the direction of our actions or thoughts. When we experience feelings such as anger, fear, jealousy, greed, impatience, judgment, or worry, our *Inner Guide* is telling us that, at that moment, we are not headed in the right direction. It is giving us a BAD feeling to tell us to change what we are doing or thinking about. Most people ignore this and remain in the action or thought and our spirit must communicate more strongly, therefore, the BAD feeling gets stronger.

In order to experience the greatest improvement in our lives, we MUST learn to follow the guidance of our *Inner Guide* and observe how we are feeling. That is the clue that tells us whether or not we are headed in the right direction. When we are feeling BAD, we must stop and look at what we are doing or thinking about and immediately change it. We must replace it with an action or thought that makes us feel GOOD. Don't wait for your *Inner Guide* to have to "yell" at you because you are coming to a dangerous part of the journey. We call that a crisis or a disaster. That is never your spirit's first option. Learn how to listen to your *Inner Guide* and you will be amazed at what you can accomplish and experience on this journey.

"In your heart you know who speaks to you and guides your life.
You need know no more. Be content to trust Spirit who guides
your every step. He will always be by your side."
- Joseph Girzone

Who Has a Better View?

Let's say you were trying to get through a maze and there was a person standing on the roof of the building across from you who could see everything from above. I'm sure you would agree that while your view is limited, he could see the proper path you should take. It would be wise to take his advice as he guided you out of this maze.

Our lives work the same way. We are all limited in our view and have access to this "man on the roof," or our spirit or *Inner Guide*. For some reason we all feel that we know where to go and will not listen to the advice of our guide, which will only lead to many dead ends. We must first admit that our views are limited and then allow ourselves to be guided. Our guide will not shout instructions from the roof but will communicate to us through our feelings, GOOD feelings means proceed, BAD feelings means change directions. We must have faith in the guidance that we are given. Remember, our guide has a better view than we do.

"When you believe that God's angels are helping you, being successful is much easier."
– John Gray

Don't Judge the "Actor"

I would like to talk about two of the most difficult challenges we face on the road to self-improvement. The first is something that we ALL do from time to time and is one of the hardest habits to break – *judging others*. It seems that whenever we look at someone else, our first thoughts are usually a judgmental thought like "they're overweight, what a silly haircut or outfit, etc.," or we'll notice the color of their skin, their religious background or even their sexual preference and send out a negative, judgmental thought. The second, and more painful challenge we face is *forgiving others*. Most people would agree that even though they might try to forgive someone who they feel has hurt them, they cannot seem to find a way to do it that truly cuts the chord that binds them. Simply saying that you forgive someone without setting them free is not really forgiving them at all.

I have a simple tip that, when applied properly, can sever the chord that keeps us bound to others through judgment and the inability to forgive. When you watch a movie and you see for example, Jack Nicholson playing a deranged character, do you get angry with him or do you realize that he is only an actor playing a role? Of course, you understand who he is, although for a short period of time, you may have forgotten who he REALLY is and mistakenly believed him to be the character he's portraying. The person that you are judging or having trouble forgiving is also just the actor playing a role. Who he really is, is spirit playing the role of that person. That character has entered your life specifically to teach you more about *non-judgment* or *forgiveness*. The problem is that you have mistakenly identified him as the "actor" he's playing. When you understand that we are ALL spirit and we are temporarily playing the roles of the people we are now, you will understand that we are truly ALL alike; we're just playing different characters in this scene. If you truly understand this, you will now know *"how"* and *"why"* you can forgive someone. You realize that he is playing his role in order for you to grow, he has done it well, and it is time to set him free.

When you look at someone who is "different" than you, instead of judging him, bless him for taking on such a unique role and subjecting himself to a difficult time here. This will provide a greater benefit to YOU than it ever could for the other person; in fact, it is one of the most empowering things you can do for yourself. I promise that if you can change the way you look at people, the world will literally change before your eyes to the wonderful stage that it truly is, where we're all performing the roles of our lifetimes.

"The thing is to see all faces as the masks of God, all characters as His roles."
- Alan Watts

The REAL Meaning of Thanksgiving and Christmas

Two of the most popular holidays observed each year are Thanksgiving and Christmas. Most people enjoy the celebrations that abound but rarely take the time to ponder their REAL meaning.

Thanksgiving is a time when we stop what we're doing and give thanks for all the good in our lives. This holiday is celebrated only once a year but should be celebrated each day for two or three minutes. We get so caught up in the drama of everyday life and give much of our attention to our problems or the things that have not gone the way we had hoped or expected that we forget to take the time to give thanks for all the wonderful things we do have. Sending out a feeling of gratitude for a few minutes each day will go a long way towards creating more things to be thankful for, as it will be attracting more "GOOD" things into your life. Remember, when you send out a positive *feeling* like gratitude, you are, at that moment, creating what shows up in your future and pulling towards you the things that you desire.

Christmas is symbolized by the giving of gifts to our loved ones. Many people may be so focused on the gifts they're going to receive that they're not even aware of the greatest gift that was already given to us two thousand years ago and is the reason we celebrate the holiday in the first place. We all know that we celebrate Christmas to commemorate the birth of Jesus Christ, who is considered either our Savior, a prophet or a simply a highly evolved human being. Whatever you believe, the fact is this holiday is celebrated by more people worldwide than any other.

The greatest gift that humanity received was the example of what is possible for every person, no matter what religion you are, no matter what sex you are and no matter what your color. Jesus taught and demonstrated through His life the power we ALL posses when you connect with your spirit and apply and work with the Universal Laws. This gift, when properly understood, is the most powerful thing ever given to man and leads to all other gifts we desire, including peace, love, joy, health, and abundance or what some would call *"Heaven on Earth."*

Always remember these two things:

1. Be grateful for all the wonderful things in your life and express that gratitude EVERY DAY.
2. KNOW what you're capable of and that we all have a hidden power that allows the impossible to become possible.

"To be happy is easy enough if we give of ourselves, forgive others, and live with thanksgiving. No self-centered person, no ungrateful soul can ever be happy, much less make anyone else happy. Life is giving, not getting."
- Joseph Fort Newton

New Day's Resolution

We have just passed a moment that does not happen very often in history. It represents the ending of many things at the same time – the end of the year, the end of the decade, the end of the century and the end of the millennium. At the same time it can represent the end of any problems or mistakes you may have endured. This moment should be looked at as the new beginning that it truly is.

Remember that what is showing up in our lives *now* has been created by our thoughts, feelings and actions of the *past*. Our *futures*, therefore, are being created by our thoughts, feelings and actions of *today*. We cannot do anything about what we may have done in the past, except learn from it and try to improve on it. We can control what we do from this moment on, though. Many people make New Year's resolutions and try to improve one area in their life and commit to changing it. Unfortunately, they usually lose their stamina by March and find themselves right back in the old habit.

This may produce a feeling of failure and may stop them from trying to improve a habit next New Year. Why not make a *"New Day's resolution"* every day and just try to get through the whole day. You'll find yourself accomplishing that goal more often, until eventually, the old habit is completely gone. This, in turn, will make you want to try to change more habits. By the time the next New Year has rolled around you'll find that instead of changing just one habit, you've changed many more and are now experiencing the benefits that come with that kind of effort. So *Happy New Day* everyone.

"The secret of health for both mind and body is not to mourn for the past, nor to worry about the future, but to live the present moment wisely and earnestly."
— Buddha

Don't Worry – Be Happy

Just hearing the words *"Don't Worry, Be Happy"* probably puts that catchy tune from the song of the same name into your head. That song was a lot more profound than you may think. It was actually sharing a Universal Truth with all of us. Worrying has been going on for so long that so many people believe that it's a way of life, or a part of being human, and that they have no control over it. That is not the case. Just because it has become such a deeply ingrained human habit does not mean we cannot release it and put an end to it.

Many people believe that if you care about someone or something, you should worry about them too, and that if you don't worry, that means you don't care. They also think that worrying will somehow make everything okay. That is not true. For some people, it becomes so bad that they start worrying about every conceivable possibility, most of which will NEVER happen. Someone once said *"Worry is like interest paid in advance on a debt that never comes due."* We must learn to differentiate between *concern* and *worry*. It's all right to be concerned for those we care about; in fact, that is actually a very loving gesture, or what can be considered a "high vibration." A "high vibration" thought or feeling will always attract a "high vibration" event into our lives, or what we call "good luck." *Worrying* is based on fear, which is considered a "low vibration." A "low vibration" thought or feeling will always produce a "low vibration" event, or what we call "bad luck." If we understood what worrying really did to us, we'd want to stop it immediately.

Remember, our natural state is one of peace and worrying keeps us from that state of peace. When that happens our spirit will try to let us know that we are off track and not headed in the direction we desire and will try to guide us back to that peaceful state. Our spirit will give us many signs to tell us to stop worrying, starting with that horrible feeling in the pit of our stomach that always accompanies worrying. When necessary, it'll use high blood pressure or even a heart attack to tell us to change that habit. We should try to listen before it gets to that level.

Mahatma Gandhi said, *"There is nothing that wastes the body like worry, and one who has any faith in God should be ashamed to worry about anything whatsoever."* Next time you find yourself worrying about something, replace that feeling with one of FAITH. Faith has the power to produce the result that you want so you don't have to experience the reality of what you're worrying about.

"Promise yourself to be so strong that nothing can disturb your peace of mind. To be too wise for worry, too tolerant for anger, and too courageous for fear. To Be Happy."
- Author Unknown

We're Human Be-ings –
Not Human Do-ings

Most people believe that in order to achieve the results we desire in life, we must work hard. *Working* is synonymous with *doing*. We think that if we DO something, that will allow us to HAVE something, which will then allow us to BE or FEEL something. In other words, we DO to HAVE to BE.

When you factor in the Law of Attraction, which is ALWAYS in effect, you come to realize that we are going about the creation process backwards. The way we FEEL is the most powerful part of the Law of Attraction—as we FEEL, we ATTRACT. Feel positive, attract positive (what we desire); feel negative, attract negative (or what we do not desire). When we DO first, we're usually doing what we think is going to make us FEEL the way we want to feel. We're following our brain's or ego's guidance and most often, we find that doesn't produce the FEELINGS we thought. What we then do is work harder, which usually makes our negative feeling of frustration grow stronger, which keeps pushing away what we truly desire. When we get into this cycle, there is not enough DOING to compensate for this type of BEING or FEELING.

How many times have you felt that in order to get what you want, you had to DO so many things; that your days seemed so full and there was no end to it all? It's almost as if you were a prisoner of your desires. In effect you are. When your life takes on that role, you've given up your freedom, which is probably your most important type of BEING. From that negative state of BEING, you will never attract the things you desire. In order to effectively create the lives we desire, or the BEINGNESS we truly want to feel, we must allow the process of creation to move in this direction:

BE ➤ HAVE ➤ DO

When you focus on your BEING, or feeling good, you will be inspired to what it is that you really want to HAVE, but this time it will be guidance from your spirit and then you will know what to DO. This is the way we find our true purpose in life, how we get to live our passion and love everyday of our lives. DOING from that state of positive BEING will attract more positive things into our lives, which will, in turn, produce more positive states of BEING and that cycle continues. This is how certain people always seem to have everything go their way.

There's an old saying that states, *"People plan and God laughs."* In other words, sometimes we must let go of our idea of how things should happen and allow our lives to unfold in a more natural way. As long as we're feeling good, what shows up will be extremely rewarding. So let's remember that we're called *"Human Beings"* for a reason. Let's try to focus more on our BEING than our DOING and, in time, we will be DOING greater, more fulfilling things than we could ever have imagined.

"Stop doing. Start being."
– Author Unknown

Pain Is an Illusion

We all experience pain in our lives, but most of the time, that pain does not exist and we suffer needlessly. Physical pain is one type of pain, and that is real. We must make the best of it and know that, in most cases, it's only temporary. The type of pain we experience most often is emotional pain, and that type of pain is an illusion, it doesn't really exist. Now you're probably saying, *"For something that doesn't exist, it sure hurts a lot. How can that be?"*

The reason we experience this type of pain is because we are trying to make our lives take a specific direction or we want to achieve certain results and our lives are not obliging. For example, what if we see someone we think is attractive but they don't like us, or if we had our heart set on a specific job but weren't hired or we just wanted something that we couldn't get? It's possible that we are being carefully guided to what's best for us, and those choices are not right for us. The greatest type of pain we go through is usually the pain of a relationship not working out. We feel that it should be a certain way and when it's not that way, we suffer tremendously. What if certain people where only supposed to be in our lives to teach us specific lessons and when they were done they would move on? If we tried to hold on to that person, we would experience pain. The reason is because we're resisting what's happening and not letting go.

Imagine you're holding on to a pole with one hand and someone is holding on to your other hand and trying to lead you in a certain direction. If you hold on to the pole, the other person will start pulling harder. The stronger your grip, the harder he pulls. Eventually, can you see how much pain you'd be in as he starts to rip you from that pole and lead you in the new direction? Who is causing the pain, him or you? YOU ARE!! How do you get the pain to disappear? By LETTING GO!!! The more resistance we give to the lessons life is trying to teach us, the more pain we will experience. Once again, this type of pain does not really exist. In fact, once we realize this, it will disappear.

By following the Law of Detachment, we will rid ourselves of most of the illusionary pain that exists in our lives. We should always try to do our best in every situation and learn the lesson that's being presented but we must not be attached to a specific result. It's when we're too attached to a specific result that we create our own pain (like holding onto that pole). When we understand that there are things going on that we may not be aware of and we stop trying to control every part of our lives, we start to flow with the current of life and as long as we don't "hold on to the pole," that current will carry us to a pain free existence.

"Suffering is simply the difference between what is and what I want it to be."
- Dr. Spencer Johnson

Tap Into Your Source...
and Find Your Passion

Through the years, we've been blessed with people who have been inspired to do great things, and we've seen and enjoyed the results of their work. For example, Mozart, Beethoven, Leonardo Da Vinci, Michelangelo and Shakespeare are a few people who come to mind that are known for creating works that are considered among the best of all time. What was their secret? How was Mozart able to play a concerto at the age of 5? How was Da Vinci able to design a helicopter 400 years before the first one was built? The answer to their secret lies hidden in the word "inspiration." The word "inspire" is derived from Latin and means *in spirit*. In other words, when they were *inspired* to do their work, they were connecting to their spirit. Understand, they were not the source of their beautiful work, they were the channels and they were just allowing their work to come through them.

We all have access to the same source that they tapped into. The spirit world is like a pool, and all we have to do is tap into that source and connect to the pool and we'll be able to do things that will amaze us. Now, I'm not saying we're all going to paint like Michelangelo or play piano like Mozart, but we will find a talent that is buried deep within us. If we can bring that talent to the surface, we can literally change our lives, as we can then begin to live our passion.

Tapping into our source is not as difficult as it may seem. We must understand that we all have two parts to ourselves— our ego and our spirit. Our ego is the temporary part of us that relates to the material world and our bodies. Our spirit is the eternal part of us, the one that exists forever and that is the part that has access to this pool. So, in order to tap into this pool, we must connect with our spirit. Our ego uses our brain to process information, make decisions and then guide us in a specific direction. Since our spirit exists forever, and our bodies do not, it's safe to say that it processes information and guides us without the brain. This is why tapping into our source and finding our passion cannot be figured out with our brain. Unfortunately, most of us are so dependent on our brain that we will never access the guidance from our spirit. Our spirit will guide us with our feelings. Whenever we feel *good*, our spirit is telling us to keep doing what we're doing. As we feel *good*, we are slowly bringing our passion to the surface. The more we feel *good*, the closer to the surface it gets. Any time you do or think about something that makes you feel *bad*, your passion is going away from the surface. The most important part of this process is to do things or think thoughts that make you feel *good*. Finding your passion is a process that will take some time, so you must be patient.

Doing what you like is freedom. Liking what you do is happiness. Make a commitment to fill your life with the freedom and happiness that comes with finding your passion.

"Whether we call it a higher power, consciousness, or the universe, there is an extraordinary source of energy and intelligence to tap into."
- Author Unknown

Inspiration or Information

Inspiration and *Information*. When you look at those words a little deeper you find something very interesting. When you break down the word "inspiration" it reads *in-spir-ation*, which is based on the word *spirit* and means that you're accessing your spirit. When you break down the word "information" it reads *in-form-ation*, which is based on the word *form*, or body, and means you're accessing your ego.

If the key to finding your passion lies in connecting to your spirit, I ask you, would you rather have *inspiration* or *information?* We are currently living in the Information Age and we are always trying to fill our brains with more and more information. Let's try to fill ourselves with more *inspiration* and we will bring ourselves into the Inspiration Age.

"O for a life of sensations rather than of thoughts!"
- John Keats

Live a Life of Balance

Life has a way of hiding so many simple truths in our everyday lives. When we see them and integrate them into our lives, the results will enhance the quality of our lives beyond measure. For example, when we drive our cars, we appreciate a smooth ride. When our car's wheels are not balanced, we will feel it; the car will give us a rough ride. It doesn't matter if it's a $100,000 car, if it's not balanced, it will not ride comfortably. That uncomfortable feeling is designed as a warning to let us know something is out of balance and if it's not put back into balance, it could lead to a serious problem.

Our lives are the same way. We all appreciate a "smooth ride." But if something is out of balance, we'll know it because we'll feel the "ride" get bumpy. That "rough ride" is the universe's way of telling us it's time to check what's out of balance and get it back into balance before a serious problem arises.

Desires are important. They lead to many of life's greatest

pleasures, if they are balanced. When the desires are out of balance, they can lead to addiction, whether it's the desire for money, sex, power, food or pleasures such as drinking and smoking. When our desires get to the point that they cannot be controlled, we will notice parts of our life start "riding rough" or maybe even falling apart in order to get our attention and get us back to a state of balance. Certain parts of our lives may be running perfectly, but at the same time we may be neglecting others, which will lead us to become unbalanced, and therefore, bring on that "rough ride" to get our attention.

For example, we may be extremely successful in our business life, but many times, it's at the expense of our personal life. In order to be successful, we may have to work very long hours and on weekends. Our ego will justify it by saying that we're building something for the future, and we just want to give our family all of the greatest things life has to offer. Well, guess what? Our children think the greatest thing life has to offer is spending time with us, and every moment spent working those extra hours could be more effectively spent with our children, giving them the attention and love they require. Many times, that "rough ride" shows up as behavioral problems, or even drug or alcohol use by the children. We may neglect the attention our body requires because we're too busy, or too lazy. Our body will definitely let us know by giving us warning signs. Those are warning signs we'll want to take care of before they become an emergency.

It's extremely important to take care of all aspects of life, including health, relationship, financial and spiritual, in a balanced manner. We should give time and attention to each part, every day, in order to ensure that our life proceeds in a smooth and balanced manner.

"The secret of life is balance, and the absence of balance is life's destruction."
- Hazrat Inayat Khau

"Why Do These Things Keep Happening to Me?"

Have you ever found yourself wondering why certain things that are usually called "bad luck" keep happening to you? It seems that the universe is just piling on one thing after another and, at that moment, you are absolutely sincere in your search for WHY they keep happening. There is a reason but the problem is that most of us don't really want to know the answer because it will destroy the way we think things work here on Earth. That is too much to handle because it would require changing many of our beliefs and habits. Most people would rather deal with the problems the universe keeps throwing at them than undergo such a radical change. If we really are sincere and would like the "bad luck" to go away, we must first admit that the way we've been taught MAY not be the way things truly are and that there may have been a few things left out. If we admit that, we now open ourselves up to learning the REAL way things work.

It's important to realize that the answers are all around

us. We are given a tremendous amount of assistance to get through this journey but we must be open and aware or we will miss them. Various ways include books that you read (like this one), movies that you watch, songs that you hear, billboards that you pass, or things people say to you. When your awareness level is high, you will find yourself asking, *"What can I learn from this? What is the message for me here?"* When you ask those questions, the answers will appear, maybe not at that moment, but in time.

The most important thing that has been left out is that, on some level, we create everything that shows up in our lives. That puts a tremendous amount of responsibility on us, but that's the only way to improve our lives. What do you think the act of Confession is all about? In its deepest form, it's about acknowledging our actions and accepting responsibility for them. Whenever we think that it's the universe or God that keeps doing these things to us, we must realize that's not the case at all. WE are doing these things to us; the universe is just doing its part. If we find that certain unpleasant things keep repeating themselves, we should ask ourselves, *"What am I being told here? What do I need to change in my life at this moment?"*

Remember, our spirits have a path that they would like us to follow. When we get too far off course, they start trying to steer us back on course. These events are designed to "straighten us out" and get us back on the path so we can get on with why we're REALLY here. Once we figure out why these things happen to us, we can then start using that knowledge to our advantage and then everybody will be saying, *"Why do these things keep happening to him/her?"* But this time they'll say it wishing it were them.

> *"The greatest griefs are those we cause ourselves."*
> – Sophocles

Pain Is One Way
the Universe Gets
Our Attention

If a mother is trying to get her child's attention, she will call out his name. If he doesn't hear her, she will speak a little louder. If he still doesn't hear her, she will speak even louder. Finally, in order to get his attention, she will be forced to scream extremely loud. At this point, the child will usually become upset and panicked because his mother is yelling at him. Whose fault is it that the mother is yelling? Of course, it's the child's. If he would have listened when his mother first called his name, she wouldn't have been forced to shout.

The universe works the same way. Many times it's trying to get our attention and is giving us information or guidance that we need to hear. It always starts off "speaking softly" but most of the time we either don't hear it or choose to ignore it. It's then forced to speak a little louder and if we continue to ignore it, like most of us do, it has no choice but to "shout loudly" at us. This can easily be avoided by simply becoming more open to the guidance we're constantly being given and by not resisting the new direction in which we're trying to be led.

We must remember that there are no accidents. Everything that happens to us is brought to us by us, on some level, in order to assist our growth process. Our spirits are trying to lead us to a state of peace and anytime we're headed in another direction, and don't hear it's initial calling, it will bring pain into our lives to get our attention so that we can change directions. Unfortunately, that's the only way many of us will listen. There are many ways the universe (spirit) will get our attention. For example, it might use an illness, a car accident, relationship problems, financial hardship, trouble with the law, or an illness (or even death) of a loved one. Generally, the more shocking or tragic the event, the louder the universe is being forced to "shout." We can be sure that before any of those events were called into our lives, we were given many opportunities to "hear" the call that was sent out. The most common choices that keep us from a state of peace are anger, fear, stress and worry. We will be given many signs to "change directions," the first being that horrible feeling that accompanies any of those. If we choose to ignore that, our lives will start to get a little bumpy, signifying that something is out of balance and we need to take care of it. If we continue to ignore it, we may start to develop high blood pressure, ulcers, or tumors. At this point, the universe is shouting at us, but not as loud as it's capable of. If we still choose to ignore it, those warning signs will lead to the full blown "shout" that it's supposed to represent, such as a stroke, heart attack or cancer. This is just one method it might choose to get our attention. As with all others, it's a gradual path that leads to that "shout." We must learn to replace *anger, fear, stress* and *worry* with *love, faith, forgiveness* and *patience*. If we do, we can heal any illness or solve any problem the universe sent to get our attention.

When the child hears the mother yelling and answers her, she will not continue to yell. Her shouting served its purpose; it got her child's attention. When you acknowledge what the universe is shouting at you, it will not need to shout any longer, it got your attention. Therefore, if you start heading in the direction you're being led and _apply_ and _demonstrate_ the principles of *love, faith, forgiveness* and *patience,* over time, those conditions will begin to heal and your life will start flowing smoothly once again.

> *"Trouble and suffering are often extremely useful because many people would not bother to learn the Truth until driven to do so by sorrow and failure."*
> - Emmet Fox

The Spiritual
Heimlich Maneuver

When someone gets something lodged in their throat and they begin to choke, the Heimlich maneuver can dislodge the obstruction and save their lives. When someone is stuck in one of life's lessons, Spirit will use extreme pain, a shocking event or tragedy, or what I call a Spiritual Heimlich Maneuver, to get our attention and help us to move forward on our path.

When we look back on our lives, we find that those hard times were what caused us to change a behavior that we had been ignoring for a long time.

"Man has the choice of learning by spiritual unfoldment or of learning by painful experience."
- Emmet Fox

Desire Everything – Need Nothing

One of the greatest feelings in life is experiencing our *desires*. They may include finding true love, raising a child, experiencing good health, having a lot of money, or owning a beautiful home, car or other material possession. These are not to be confused with our *needs*, which include food to eat, water to drink, air to breathe and money to pay our essential bills. One of the biggest problems we run into in life is when we allow our *desires* to become *needs*. When this happens, we begin to start pushing away the very thing we desire.

For example, if you *desire* someone's love, respect or attention and you don't receive it, you may not be happy but you'll be okay with it. But if you *need* someone's love, respect or attention and you don't receive it, you'll be very upset and your actions will show it. How do you think that will affect the way the other person acts towards you now? This is how many arguments start. They could easily be avoided when the *need* for love, respect or attention is turned into a *desire*.

Many people get into financial trouble when they confuse their *desires* with their *needs*. You may *desire* to buy that new car, TV, outfit or whatever else it may be, but you probably don't *need* it. If you think you *need* it, you'll probably buy it without thinking and get yourself into debt. Understanding that it's a *desire* and not a *need* will give you the patience to wait for the right time before you make the purchase. Of course, we have the physical pleasures such as sex, drinking, and smoking. When we mistake our *desire* for those with a *need*, we definitely have to stop and re-evaluate the direction our lives are headed in.

The only reason we *need* something from someone else is because we think it must be missing and the other person will fill that void. If we just realized that we're already perfect and we allowed that perfection to rise to the surface and begin to show itself, we would not *need* so many things to help make us feel better. Many people spend their lives searching outside of themselves for the things they think will give them the inner peace they so desire. Unfortunately, they never bother to look in the one place where it can be found – inside of them.

The greatest treasures of life can be found when you change the direction of your search from an outer to an inner journey. When you do, you will understand the difference between *desires* and *needs*. You will then find all of your *needs* being met and you'll get to experience and enjoy all of your greatest *desires*.

"Peace comes from within. Do not seek it without."
– Buddha

Which Voice Do I Listen To?

All of us have heard the voice that speaks to us inside our heads. Many times we depend on that voice to help guide us through certain difficult situations. Sometimes we've listened to that voice and the results were not what we had hoped they'd be. We've also experienced times when we heard two voices giving us different advice. How can we learn to distinguish which voice to listen to? First, we must understand what each voice represents. One voice represents our ego and the other represents our spirit. Our ego and our spirit have different agendas; therefore, the guidance they give will be different.

The ego is always trying to protect us from things it thinks can hurt us. The spirit knows its true essence, that it is eternal, therefore nothing can hurt it. The ego thinks we are all separate individuals and that we are competing with everybody else for a limited amount of love, money, time, attention, etc. The spirit knows we are all connected and that there is enough of everything.

The ego believes in WIN/LOSE; the spirit believes only in WIN/WIN. The ego believes the illusion called "Life on Earth" is all there is; the spirit knows that this life is only a small part of our TRUE existence.

The ego focuses on the past and future, which do not exist. It regrets or feels guilty about the past, is worried about or fears the future and thinks it can't be happy until a future event happens. The spirit lives in the present moment, which is the only one that exists. When you are in the present moment, you'll notice that everything is okay and no matter what may be going on in your life at the time, there is really nothing to fear. The ego knows that as long as you're focusing on the past or future, you don't have time to live in the present moment. It's in the present moment that you have access to spirit, and your true power. If you accessed that power, your ego would be out of a job, so it must tell you these things to keep itself in business.

The ego will say things like, *"I can't do that...I'm not ready...I don't have enough training...There's no way it will work...What's in it for me?...What if I fail?...He/she'll never like me...What will everyone think?...I'm better than he/she is...He/she is such a jerk... etc."*

The spirit will say things like, *"I can do that...I may not know everything about it but I will start now...I can make it work...How will it help others?....What if it succeeds?...He/she will like me...I know what I'm doing is right, I'm not concerned with what the others think...He/she and I may not agree but I think he/she is okay...etc."*

We must be aware of what we're focusing on and what that little voice inside is telling us and we'll know what part of ourselves we're accessing, our higher self (spirit) or lower self (ego). When we know that, we can then choose to always come from our higher self and follow the Divine guidance we're being given and we'll start creating a First Class life.

"The Spirit is the true self."
– Cicero

How to Get Past
the Guard at the Door

Have you ever had trouble trying to communicate with someone you care about? You're trying to get a point across but you realize they're totally closed to what you're saying. Or they say they understand your point but you realize they're just not "getting it." It's obvious that the message is getting lost somewhere between where the words leave your mouth to the time they get to the other person's brain. This type of communication breakdown is extremely common and is the main cause of problems in a relationship, whether it's romantic, friendship, family or business.

The way to solve this problem is to understand what's really happening. To help make this clear, I'll use the following analogy:

Let's say there is a prisoner locked in a room that has a guard at the door and you would like to get a message to the prisoner. You would have to give the message to the guard and he would relay it to the prisoner. You later find out that the prisoner did not receive the message so you give another message to the guard, hoping that he'll deliver it this time. He says that he will but you find out that, once again, he did not deliver the message. At this point you realize that you must find another way of delivering the message and that you must bypass the guard and go directly to the prisoner. Only then, will he get the message that you're trying to give him.

The prisoner that you're tying to get the message to is the person's spirit and the guard at the door is the person's ego. When someone is having a communication breakdown, or a full blown argument, it's usually because the person's ego has stepped up to protect the individual because he feels he's being attacked. That's what the ego is supposed to do. It believes it is alone and must defend itself when being attacked with the primary goal being to win, and if that means someone else loses, so be it. What's happening is that the ego is not delivering the message you're trying to communicate to the spirit, which is the part of that person that wants peace. The spirit knows it is not alone, that we are all one, and only wants a situation where everyone wins and nobody loses.

Knowing this, you must now find a way to get the message directly to the spirit, and bypass the ego. The way do this, very simply, is through prayer. When you are alone, silently speak to the other person's spirit and communicate the message you're trying to get across. This doesn't require much effort, just a little time and patience. Don't expect to have it work after one try; that will only lead to disappointment. You must give it a chance to take effect but I guarantee you will be amazed at how effective you'll find this can be.

When we look back through history, we find that *win/lose* situations only provide temporary solutions. We must seek to find *win/win* situations that can move individuals and society to a state of peace. The only way to do that is to bypass the "guard at the door" and get the message to people's spirits.

"A prayer in its simplest form is merely a wish turned Godward."
– Phillips Brooks

60 Seconds for 60 Days

Here is a simple, but extremely effective technique that can transform people, relationships and situations before your very eyes. Think of something you want to change. It could be someone you care about who is having a problem, whether it be personal, financial or health related. It could be someone you're having trouble communicating with lately or it could be a situation that seems to have gotten off track. Hold that person or situation in your mind for 60 seconds and pray that the spirits of all involved help heal this situation. Do this everyday for 60 days and watch what happens.

As a reminder, put a Post-It note on your refrigerator that says, "*60 seconds for 60 days.*" Do not discuss this with anyone, as this will dilute the energy that is required to fulfill the command. The Power of Prayer is real and we all have access to it. If we learn how to use it properly, we will experience miracles that will amaze us.

"A day hemmed in prayer is less likely to unravel."
– Author Unknown

Sandcastles by the Shore

We have all been in situations where life has gotten to be so difficult, nothing is happening the way we would like it to. Everything seems to be falling apart and we finally cry out to God for help. It's as if we've tried everything we could and we're finally coming to Him for help because we realize that we can't do it by ourselves. Unfortunately, that's the time most of us start making prayer a part of our lives. That's like asking for directions after we've already gotten lost. If we would have just asked for directions before we started the trip, we would not have gotten lost.

Life could be a lot easier if we made prayer a part of our everyday lives and just talked to God more often. There are a few things we should know about prayer that would make it more effective. For example, why are some prayers answered while some are not? Prayer is a force that works with our true reality, not with our illusionary world. Most of the structures we have built in our lives are part of our temporary illusion, not our true reality. When our illusions start to fall apart, we come to God for help and He seems to ignore us.

An analogy I'll use is when a child makes a sandcastle by the shore. The child may spend hours building the most beautiful sandcastle but when the tide comes in, the sandcastle will be destroyed. If the child were to cry to his father to help save the sandcastle, the father would tell him that the sandcastle was only temporary, it was not meant to be permanent.

The things we create in our lives, whether it's our careers, relationships, material possessions, etc., are our "sandcastles." When those structures start falling apart, we cry to God to help save them. The reason why that type of prayer won't be answered is because He is telling us that that particular structure was only supposed to be temporary; it was not meant to be permanent. If we are attached to the illusion and try to hold on to that structure, we will experience tremendous pain and it will seem as if our prayers were not answered. Knowing this, we must learn to pray on the dimension of reality. Our spirit lives on the dimension of reality and if something is asked for that is for the advancement of our spirit, it will be answered.

For example, instead of praying to keep a relationship going, ask God for whatever is for the highest good of both people involved and that you both understand the lesson that the relationship is trying to teach. When someone is extremely ill, don't ask that they be healed. That may not be for their highest good, and, therefore won't be answered. The illness may have been created to help teach that person something, so ask God to help that person learn the lesson that's being presented so they can then be healed. When you desire a relationship with someone in particular, more money, a specific material object or career path, always ask for it *only if it's for your highest good* and accept whatever happens.

From now on, when asking God for help, ask yourself first if you are praying to enhance your reality or to have him save your "sandcastle."

"All prayers are answered when the individual doesn't tell God how to answer them."
- Edgar Cayce

"God, Please Help Me!"

How many times have we asked God for help when we were suffering and seemed to be backed into a corner with no chance of escape? We promise God that if He just helps us out of this jam, we'll "never do that again," we'll change the behavior that needs changing and we'll make more time in our lives for Him. But once He's helped us, we seem to forget who it was that got us out of the jam. We think we got ourselves out and we go back on our promise. Time goes by and before you know it, we find ourselves backed into that same corner. Guess who we call again to help us out? That's right, God.

What's my point here? Two things. First, let's not forget who it is that's getting us out of that painful corner. We should show Him more gratitude for the assistance He's given us. Second, let's keep our promises we made and change our behavior and include Him in our lives more often. If we want to stay out of that painful corner and have our lives flow more smoothly, don't just call on God when you need Him. Start having a relationship with God and He'll be the best friend you have.

"If we really want to pray, we must first learn to listen, for in the silence of the heart God speaks."
– Mother Teresa

Have FAITH – FEAR Not

One of the greatest challenges we face on the path of life is facing our fears. At times, our fears can literally paralyze us and totally disrupt our lives. Unfortunately for most people, our fears have tremendous power over us. But when properly understood, we can all "pull the plug" on that power and reclaim the wonderful reality that is possible for everyone.

FEAR stands for _False_ _Evidence_ _Appearing_ _Real_. In other words, whatever we fear is just an illusion that only _seems_ real. When we send out a fear response, we have just told the universe that we believe this to be real and we literally give that illusion energy and pull it towards us until it becomes real in our lives. For example in the movie, _"The Wizard of Oz,"_ when Dorothy and her friends went to see the Wizard at the castle, they found him to be a tremendous image with a loud booming voice that had smoke coming from it, which instilled a tremendous amount of fear in all of them. They felt powerless until the dog, Toto, went behind the curtain and revealed that the Wizard was just a small man, speaking into a microphone and pulling on a bunch of levers. Once they realized this illusion, the image that they feared lost all of its power over them.

Our everyday fears are the same, although, on the surface they may appear to be real. Once we understand that we give them power with our fear response, all we have to do is acknowledge that it's just an illusion and replace the FEAR vibration with a FAITH vibration. I know that it's not an easy thing to do, but the results will far outweigh the effort.

FAITH stands for _For_ _All_ _Is_ _Truly_ _Harmonious_. Once we become aware that beneath the surface, all is perfectly calm, we then bring that peace to the surface and have it show up in our lives. It's easy to demonstrate faith when things are going our way, but the real test comes when a situation arises that causes us to react with fear. When you consistently demonstrate faith you will find that you literally conquer every illusionary fear that crosses your path.

Voltaire said, _"Faith consists in believing when it is beyond the power of reason to believe."_ In other words, don't listen to what your mind is telling you is real, it does not have access to the TRUE reality. Tap into that part of you that can see beneath the surface and watch all of your fears dissolve right in front of your eyes.

> _"Fear creates an imaginary wall in your life which limits your vision. That fear is an illusion. Walk through that wall and behold the beauty that awaits you."_
> - Andrew Moss

Grains of Sand

One of the most important tools required for our journey here on Earth is money. Money represents the energy we exchange in order to receive certain things to make our lives more comfortable such as shelter, food, clothing, transportation, medicine, as well as many other pleasures. Everybody would like to have enough to get their needs met and many of us would like to have much more so that we could enjoy more of life's pleasures that depend on money.

We live in an abundant universe and the Scriptures say that we can all experience this wonderful abundance. For some reason, though, many people struggle to have their needs met while others seem to always have more than enough. If we can figure out how to tap into that abundant supply the universe has waiting for us, more of us will be able to experience that abundance and enjoy the benefits that accompany it.

First, let's look at why people do not have abundance in

their lives. Remember, we are always creating what is showing up in our lives by our thoughts and feelings, or consciousness. If we have an abundance consciousness, we will have an abundant supply provided. On the other hand, if we have a scarcity consciousness, that is what will show up in our lives. Most of us are taught that there is not enough in this world, whether it is money, food, love, etc. As a result, we have developed a scarcity consciousness that keeps us experiencing that feeling of not having enough by stopping the flow of abundance the universe is waiting to pour upon us.

How can we change from a scarcity to an abundance consciousness? By first changing our beliefs. First understand that there is more than enough money for everyone. Remember, the source of all money is not here on the physical plane (Earth) but on the universal or spiritual plane. In that plane, money has no value; it only has value here on Earth. So, to the universe, money is like grains of sand and there is an infinite supply. All we have to do is ask and, if it's for our highest good, the money will begin to flow to us. For example, if a father has a lot of money, he will not give his child money every time he asks because sometimes there is a lesson that must be learned first, like responsibility.

The Bible says, *"Ask and you shall receive."* Many of you are saying, *"I've asked, how come I've never received?"* That's because you've asked but you didn't really believe that there was enough and that you would get any of it. The universe always knows your core thoughts and your life is created based on those thoughts. Once you understand that the universe has an unlimited "sea of money" that is just waiting for you to claim, get your sand pail and shovel ready because those "grains of sand" are on their way.

"You must have faith to succeed, because if you're without faith, you're without hope."
– Napoleon Hill

Claim Your Trust Fund

Imagine if you just found out that a long lost relative left you a fortune in a trust fund that was just waiting for you to claim. Could you think of anything better? We all have a trust fund waiting for us that the universe (our Father) has left us that is waiting for us to claim. How do we claim this trust fund? The answer is in the name itself, TRUST. When we truly *trust* or have *faith* that it is there and waiting for us to claim, we will be allowed access to it.

> *"Faith is affirming success before it comes. Faith is making claims to victory before it is achieved."*
> - Robert Schuller

The Power of the Spoken Word

We are all more powerful than we can imagine. Most of us are not even aware of one of the most powerful ways we create our reality everyday and that's by the use of our words. The words we speak paint the pictures that will appear in our lives, and the emotion that we feel as we speak them is the energy that is contoured and formed into our reality.

For example, when we tell everyone how sick we are, we are speaking those words to the universe and they are being fueled by the emotion that's behind them. A statement with a congruent feeling, or core thought, is a command to the universe and the universe has no option but to create that scenario. When you say, *"I'm sick...my back hurts...I have a headache...etc.,"* the universe grants your command. If you happen to be sick, don't tell everybody how sick you are. Try to remain quiet and you will find yourself feeling better much sooner.

This also applies to your financial situation. Whenever you say, *"I don't have enough money,"* or *"I can't afford it,"* you're telling the universe what reality to create and you're keeping yourself in that situation. Instead, try saying, *"I choose not to buy this at this time."* If things are not going your way financially, don't share that with others because every time you do, you chain that situation to you. The more times you repeat the story, the more frustrated you get about being in that situation, so your emotion gets stronger and, in effect, the chain also gets stronger and harder to break.

When you talk about what's wrong in your life, you bring up negative emotions. The combination of your words and emotions create more of "what's wrong." When you talk about what's right in your life, you create more of "what's right." So spend more time talking about all the things that are right in your life. You will notice that if you look for them, you will find many things that are going your way and more to be grateful for.

When life is not going our way, we are usually depleted of our energy. What we want at that moment is more energy, and it usually doesn't matter what form it takes. Most of us love to share our problems because we receive energy from other people when we can play the victim and they feel sorry for us. In fact, we've found that energy to be easier to get so we choose that before we try to get ourselves out of the uncomfortable situation we're in. That's a Band-aid solution; it doesn't solve the problem, it just makes us feel better temporarily.

Instead of saying, *"I can't wait,"* say, *"I'm looking forward to..."* That demonstrates patience to the universe, which will allow what you desire to come to you much more quickly. Stop speaking in the negative. Don't say things like, *"I better not lose my keys,"* or *"I hope I do not fail this test."* The universe does not pick up the negative, it only responds to what you said (lose my keys, fail this test), so you'll increase the chances of losing your keys or failing the test. Once we realize we possess this power and the results we are creating with it everyday, we will start respecting that power and using it responsibly.

"The happiness of your life depends upon the quality of your thoughts (words)."
– Marcus Antonius

Why Do We Get Sick?

At different points in our lives, most of us will have to deal with a temporary physical breakdown, or sickness. Believe it or not, sickness serves a very valuable purpose in our lives, one that will become clear when you understand the real reason why we get sick.

First you must remember that everything originates from the spiritual dimension (cause) and then manifests in the physical dimension (effect). If we know where the cause lies, we can help cure the effect. Today, most people, including the medical profession, are looking for the causes of diseases on the physical level, but as you will find out, that's not where they lie.

For example, most people think the cause for giving birth is that a man and a woman have sex; his sperm fertilizes her egg and she gets pregnant. That is not the *cause*. The primary cause is that a spirit needs a body to host its incarnation and the physical process I just described is the way spirit accomplishes that. Biology is just the way spirit gets things done in the physical world.

Before the spirit chooses a body, it realizes that the host will probably not be aware of it. It has to try to help navigate this physical host through its journey on the physical plane and will do so by communicating to it in various ways. One way it communicates is through feelings. It gives us a "good" feeling when it wants us to proceed in a certain direction or it gives us a "bad" feeling when it wants us to change directions. This could be for our thoughts or our actions, although actions are just our thoughts made manifest.

When we ignore those directions, it uses another form of communication, the physical body. The spirit will bring an ailment upon a particular part of the body in order to tell us something specific about what area we need to change our direction. For example, a fever means we are holding in anger towards something. A cold means we have too much going on at one time and we are wearing ourselves out. The body shuts down and forces us to rest. Constipation means we are holding on to old ideas that it may be time to get rid of. High blood pressure means we are holding on to an old emotional wound and we're being told to let go of it. Cold sores mean we have a fear of expressing angry words. If we speak what's on our mind, the condition can heal. Cancer means we've been holding on to a long-standing resentment that has been eating away at us. (For more details about the metaphysical reasons for illness and affirmations to help heal these conditions, refer to the book "Heal Your Body" by Louise Hay.)

Another way our spirit communicates to us is through our children or pets. Spirit understood that sometimes we would care more about them than ourselves and uses them to communicate a specific message. Children and animals are very receptive to energy and as we bring our negative energy home with us and shower it all over our children and pets, they will develop the sickness which is telling us to change our thoughts and actions. For example, earaches in children mean that there's too much anger around and the parents may be arguing too much. Cancer in a pet means that we are infecting its space with too much anger and stress and we must stop focusing on the thoughts that are creating that anger and stress.

What about diseases that we are genetically predisposed to, or that run in the family? It's not guaranteed that we will develop that disease. We chose a body with that predisposition for a reason. That is a card that Spirit holds waiting to deal, if necessary. In other words, if we're not making the progress of which we're capable. If we learn the spiritual lesson we're in, that card will not have to be dealt and we will not get that disease.

As much as most people are trying to deny their spiritual nature, eventually we will be forced to face the fact that we are spirit first. Sickness and disease are something we will have to deal with until that time. If you believe that we were created in the image and likeness of God and that God does not get sick, then you'll agree that we were not created with the intention of getting sick; that was brought on as a method of correction once humanity got "off the path" and forgot its true nature.

In order to experience the perfect health that we're meant to have, we must listen to what we're being told and change what we're being asked to change. I believe very strongly in the medical profession's ability to treat the *effects* of diseases but I believe we can do a lot better when it comes to dealing with the *causes*. Obviously there is no money to be made for the medical profession and pharmaceutical companies in treating the cause, but that's a whole other story (another part of the illusion...).

> *"Great men are they who see that spiritual is stronger than any material force, that thoughts rule the world."*
> – Ralph Waldo Emerson

Follow the "Flow of Life"

So many of us are sincerely trying to find an easier way to get through life. Deep down inside of us there is a voice that tells us, *"It doesn't have to be this hard. Life was not meant to be such hard work."* That voice is correct. The only reason life is so difficult for most of us is because we unknowingly keep working against ourselves because we don't understand the way life REALLY works.

So how does life REALLY work? I'm glad you asked.

First, it's important to understand that everything is made up of vibrations and when two vibrations match, they will be *"in flow,"* when they don't, they'll be *"out of flow."* You'll know the difference by the feeling you get as you go through your day. When everything seems to be going against you and you feel like you're using a great deal of effort to make things work, you're *"out of flow."* When things seem to fall into place without effort and you seem to be in a great mood, then you're *"in flow."* I'm sure you can remember experiencing both.

So the next question is, "How do we fall *"out of flow?"* (Boy, you keep asking the right questions!) The only reason you get *"out of flow"* after a period of being *"in flow"* is because you've allowed something to affect the way you feel, thus changing your vibration, which leaves you *"out of flow"* with the current you had been floating on. We always make the mistake of allowing outside events to determine the way we feel, without realizing the consequences.

The amount of effort you expend in life is directly related to the current of the "flow of life" you follow. The higher your vibration, or the better you feel, the more *"in flow"* you'll be and less effort will be required to get you through daily life. The lower your vibration, or the worse you feel, the more *"out of flow"* you'll be, which means you will require more effort to do what you want to do.

For example, if you're paddling a boat through a river and you follow the current, you can coast and allow the flow to carry you, or you can paddle and get even better results. Either way, it will feel effortless as you travel down the river. But if you decide to go against the current, it will require much more effort to reach your destination.

We must control the way we feel, regardless of what's happening in our outer world, and we can then begin to control the flow of our own lives. Just as a captain is in charge of steering a ship, we should all take charge of steering our own vessel through the sea of life. When we do, it'll be smooth seas ahead.

"All the frictions, all the uncertainties, all the ills, the sufferings, the fears, the forebodings, the perplexities of life come to us because we are out of harmony with the divine order of things."
- Ralph W. Trine

How We Create Our Reality

For those of you who believe that we create our reality and really want to understand HOW, I will break it down in simple terms so you can try to incorporate these ideas into your life and take control of what's showing up. For those of you that don't believe it, who feel that's just too much responsibility to handle, you can skip this section, put your head back in the sand and go back to your everyday life hoping things *miraculously* get better.

First, you must realize that there is nothing in your life that you are NOT creating. (Yes, that certainly puts a lot of responsibility on your shoulders.) In other words, you are creating EVERYTHING that shows up, both "good" and "bad." When you understand HOW, you can create more "good" than "bad."

Everything in this world and in the universe is made up of vibrations. What appears to us as solid, such as ice, is nothing more than molecules vibrating at a particular speed. When you speed up the vibration it becomes water and if you speed it up some more it becomes steam. Our thoughts have their own distinct vibration; thoughts that *feel "good"* have a higher vibration than thoughts that *feel "bad."*

Now, the *Law of Attraction* states that similar vibrations will attract each other. High vibration (good) thoughts will attract high vibration (good) events; just as low vibration (bad) thoughts will attract low vibration (bad) events.

Our reality is like a holographic ball of clay, it appears to be real but it's formed and sculpted based on the vibration we give off. We are giving off a vibrational signal AT ALL TIMES. Whenever we are focusing on something, we are giving off a specific vibrational signal. For example, when we are thinking or talking about something, we are giving off a signal; when we are remembering something, we are offering a signal; when we are imagining something, we are giving off a signal. The universe is constantly matching our signal with things of a similar vibration. *As we think, we vibrate. As we vibrate, we attract.*

The most important thing to realize is that what we focus on and what comes back to us is ALWAYS a vibrational match. The reason something wonderful happens in our life is because we are a vibrational match to that; the reason something terrible happens in our life is because, once again, that is a vibrational match to the signal we're offering. Now we're starting to understand that WE are the source of everything that is showing up in our lives. The universe is just doing its part, using the Law of Attraction, and matching what we're giving off.

In order to change what's showing up in our lives, we must change the signal that we're offering. We do that by monitoring what we're focusing on – thinking about, talking about, remembering and imagining – at ALL times. Now, I'm sure you're thinking, *"It's pretty tough to monitor all that – all the time."* I agree that it is difficult but we have help to make it easier. When we were created, we were given an Internal Guidance System that would help us monitor what we were focusing on. Our Creator gave us the power of creation (we are made in the image and likeness of God) and that creative power is our thoughts. He understood that unchecked thoughts are like unharnessed energy – powerful but dangerous. So we were given a system to make sure that we used that power effectively. That Internal Guidance System is our _feelings_. Our feelings are designed to let us know when we are using our creative powers to our advantage and when we are using them to our detriment. When we _feel "good,"_ our Guidance System is telling us that what we are creating is something that we will want; when we _feel "bad,"_ our Guidance System is telling us that we are using our creative powers to create what we don't want and that we must change what we are focusing on. The reason why it feels so bad is so that we will not want to remain in that feeling and the only way to change that feeling is to change what we're focusing on. It's the same reason we get burned when we touch something hot; if we do not remove our hand we will damage our skin. The burning sensation is designed to get us to move. Just the same, the negative feelings we experience are designed to get us to change our thoughts before we experience what we create.

So remember these points:

1. Everything in the universe has a vibration, including our thoughts.
2. We create EVERYTHING that shows up in our lives. Our thoughts are our _creative power._
3. By the Law of Attraction, the universe is always matching the vibrational signal we're offering.
4. Our _feelings_ are our Internal Guidance System letting us know when we should change what we're focusing on.

When we truly understand how this works and start consciously creating what's showing up in our lives, we will be amazed at what we're capable of. That's when life becomes a constant miracle.

"All that we are is the result of what we have thought. If a man speaks or acts with an evil thought, pain follows him. If a man speaks or acts with a pure thought, happiness follows him, like a shadow that never leaves him."
- Buddha

Find the Hidden Pearl

"How can I get rid of the problems in my life?" I'm sure we've all asked that question before. Wouldn't it be nice to know the answer? Now that you've read the previous story (if you haven't, read it now), and you understand that you are creating everything that is showing up in your lives, you're on your way to finding the answer.

The only reason that a "problem" is in your life is to teach you something. Hidden inside every "problem" is a pearl of wisdom. That pearl may be any of the following: patience, non-judgment, forgiveness, acceptance, love, a change of directions in life, realizing our true essence – that we are all powerful and eternal, to name a few. Once you find the pearl, the "problem" disappears. It will either not show up in your life again or you will not see it as a problem any more. So the answer to the question, *"How can I get rid of the problems in my life?"* is simply: FIND THE HIDDEN PEARL.

Now the question is, *"How do I find the hidden pearl?"* Finding the hidden pearl requires three steps:

1. *Accept responsibility.* Whatever the situation is, we must understand that WE created it. Without this step, we can NOT solve the problem. It's so much easier initially to play the victim and not take responsibility, but in the long run, it's much more difficult because the problems will keep showing up and actually get bigger each time. Some people feed off of the energy of playing the victim and having people feel sorry for them. This is an addiction that must be shed in order to improve one's life.

2. *Bless the situation.* Once you understand that you created the situation to teach you something (in order to receive that pearl of wisdom), you can bless it for the gift that it truly represents. When you judge the situation as "bad" and fight it, you actually give it energy and it grows in your life. It's like adding fuel to a fire. Remember, what you resist persists. When you bless the situation, you feed it a completely different type of energy, like adding water to the fire, and the problem disappears, bringing you one step closer to revealing the hidden pearl.

3. *Surrender.* When you surrender to the situation, you change the negative energy of resistance and judgment, which is like the smoke keeping the pearl hidden, into a neutral energy, which clears the smoke and reveals the pearl.

One situation this can be helpful with is if someone is lying on their deathbed, afraid to die. Applying these three steps can change their transition. First, accept responsibility knowing that life was created with transition as part of the design; we all go through it. Then, do not fight the situation, but bless it, knowing that something wonderful awaits on the other side of the veil. And finally, surrender to what is taking place, let go of this life and your pearl will be revealed. (Why do you think they call it *"The Pearly Gates?"*)

You can apply these three steps to all of the "problems" that show up in your life, whether they pertain to relationships, your health, or your finances. When you do, your "problems" will disappear and be replaced by challenges that reveal a treasure of hidden pearls.

"There is no such thing as a problem without a gift for you in its hands. You seek problems because you need their gifts."
- Richard Bach

— Part 2—

Hidden Treasures

On the surface, these parables are entertaining stories, but beneath the surface lie the "hidden treasures" which provide a deeper glimpse of "reality."

The Dream

There once was this being that lived a perfect life. He always experienced the greatest pleasures you could ever think of. There was no sickness or pain; in fact, it was filled with all the things he ever wanted.

One day, he woke up in a strange place; he did not know where he was. The perfect place he once knew seemed like a distant memory he barely remembered. He was very frustrated because he could not communicate easily with anyone. For some strange reason, he was extremely clumsy and could not even walk. In fact, he had to learn to do virtually everything in order to survive. As time went on, he learned how to walk and talk. He learned the difference between pleasure and pain, good and bad and love and hate. All of this was new to him because they did not exist in the place he was before; everything was just perfect. But all of these experiences helped him grow and become the person he became.

As time went on, he grew into a beautiful person. When he first arrived in this new place, his stay was made a lot more comfortable because two special people helped care for him. Eventually, he got acclimated to his new surroundings and was able to take care of himself. When the time came, he returned that loving gesture and took care of them. One day, he found himself on his own. By now, he understood the way things worked in this place and he found that he fit right in with everyone else. His path led him to someone that brought out a feeling he never experienced in this new place before. It was very exciting and he decided to stay with this person and travel the path together. Over the next few years, they experienced the miracle of giving life four times. Together, the two of them helped shape the lives of these four young children, but as time went on, he felt he had to take a different path. Once again, he was on his own.

One day, he was enjoying the sun and the ocean with his children, when he saw the most beautiful person he had ever seen. He had experienced something like this before but he did not remember it being this strong. Luckily, he gathered up the courage to talk to this "angel of beauty" and he realized that she was experiencing the same feelings as he was. He knew he would not be traveling this path alone anymore; he now had a companion. Over time, he shared the miracle of giving life four times with his new life partner. Together, they helped these four children become beautiful adults. Once again, though, the signs showed him it was time to walk the path alone. So his journey continued, his family never being too far away.

He found that each part of his journey provided him with the opportunity to experience every type of feeling; every type of pleasure and every type of pain, but that's what made the journey so special.

One day he started to notice that things were not as easy as they once were. The little things he used to do automatically now required a great deal of effort. He started experiencing pains that he never had before. He realized that his journey would soon be coming to an end. His family was nearby and helped take care of him and prepare him for the end of the journey. He was scared because he did not know what to expect, but something inside him told him everything would be OK. He said his good-byes to everybody and closed his eyes. A beautiful peace came over him as he drifted off.

All of a sudden, he woke up and he was back where he was before the journey began. He was back in the perfect place. He was exactly the same as he was before; it was as if he had never left. He then realized that the journey was a dream and that he just woke up. Everything that he experienced, all the greatest pleasures and most terrifying pains, were all just a dream. He realized that no matter what happened in that dream, though, he was now back in the world of the perfect, where everything is, and always will be, PERFECT.

- FOR DAD

"Life is like a dream, When you wake up…it's over."
- Andrew Moss

The Hidden Power

Once upon a time, in a land not too far away, lived a man named Johnny. Johnny was a normal guy; he was healthy, had a good job, a good relationship with his family and friends and pretty much anything a man could ask for. Johnny always knew there was something more to life but he didn't know what it was. He kept following what the familiar voice in his head told him. "I know what you want and I'll show where it is. I'm here to protect you and lead you to what's best for you. Don't worry, just do what I tell you." Johnny always listened; he never questioned what he was told to do. Everywhere Johnny went and everything he did always led to a dead end. He would get what the voice told him he wanted but it never truly satisfied him. The voice would then tell him, "If that didn't satisfy you then this surely will." This cycle continued for many years and it did bring him many temporary pleasures and certainly made his life exciting but he knew there was still something missing.

Johnny kept hearing about the "*Hidden Power*" that could change his life and decided to find out where it was. He asked everyone he could where this *Hidden Power* could be found but they always responded, "I heard of it but I don't know where it is." Not a day went by that Johnny did not think of it. His search led him to far away places, always hoping that it was bringing him closer to the *Hidden Power*.

One day, someone said, "I know of the Power that you speak of. You must climb that mountain that you see in the distance and a wise old man will be sitting there waiting for you. He knows of your search and can help you find what you seek." Johnny was so excited because he knew his quest was nearing an end and he couldn't wait to experience the benefits and riches that were promised to those who had the *Hidden Power*. He followed the trail and ran up the mountain. The steeper the climb, the more determined he became. Nothing could stop him now.

Finally, he reached the top and just as he was told, an old wise man sat there in silence. "I'm told you can lead me to the *Hidden Power*," Johnny said.

"Yes I can," the wise man replied.

"Is it up here on the top of this mountain?" Johnny asked.

The wise man spoke softly, "Sit down and listen to me now. The clue to finding this *Power* lies in the answer to this riddle. *The Power that you search for is both near and far. It is hidden in a place that is closer than you think and farther than you can imagine, but first you must find the key that will unlock the door to where it is hidden.*"

Johnny realized that the *Power* was not up on that mountain, so he thanked the wise man and continued his search more determined than ever.

After searching all over and trying so hard to find it, he found his life crumbling around him and he cried out in pain. He was lying in silence, tears running down his face, when he heard a faint voice speak out, one that he had not heard before. "Can you hear me?"

"Yes I can," he answered.

"Good. I've been trying to get your attention for a long

time but you wouldn't listen. You were always doing things your own way so I had to create a bit of pain in your life in order for you to stop and hear me. You must understand that you could have chosen to listen to me at any time and the pain would not have been so great."

"Who are you?" Johnny asked.

"I am you," the voice replied.

"I don't understand," Johnny said.

"Of course not. Nobody ever does…at first. You are not the *real* you, you are the *temporary* you. I am the REAL you. I have been patiently waiting until the right time when you would be able to listen to me and we could begin to work together."

"You mean we're supposed to work together?" Johnny asked.

"Yes. You see, I am the key that is required to unlock the door to the *Power* that you seek. Have you figured out where that *Power* is hidden?"

"I've searched everywhere. I've been to all the holy places, the places with the greatest energy, everywhere I could think where it might be hidden and I could not find it," Johnny replied.

"I'll give you one more clue. *As far as you've traveled you got no closer to it and no further from it. It's the one place no one will ever look because they cannot see it.*"

Johnny thought and thought, deeper than he ever had before. He closed his eyes and felt himself connecting with his REAL self when a bright light went on that almost blinded him. He couldn't understand what it was because his eyes were still closed.

"I GOT IT!" he screamed. "I can see this beautiful, bright light but my eyes are closed. I believe the *Power* that I've been searching for is not 'out there' but inside of me."

"Very good. You have found it. Now we must work together to be sure that we use this *Power* responsibly. The temporary you has different needs and desires than the REAL you and this *Power* is not to be used for those things. It can be very dangerous so you are not allowed access to it until you have connected to the REAL you. And now you have earned that access."

And so it was that Johnny found the greatest treasures in all of life, the one's that can only be acquired with the *Hidden Power*

"Within you now is the power to do things you never dreamed possible. This power becomes available to you as soon as you change your beliefs."
- Dr. Maxwell Maltz

Planting Seeds

In a small town, just outside of the Big City, lived a normal man who led an average life. He worked about ten hours a day, six days a week, as did most of the people of this beautiful town. Every day, after work, while everybody was home doing what most people do after work – watch TV, hang out with their friends, have a beer, or take a nap, this guy would get in his car, drive off and not return until hours later. All of his friends kept asking what he was doing but all he ever said was "PLANTING SEEDS." Nobody ever saw him actually go and plant these seeds. They just figured he was a strange guy with weird habits.

Ten years went by and his friends were still working hard, struggling with their lives and "problems." One day, they ran into their friend and realized he was so at peace and seemed very happy. They said he looked like a new man and they asked him how he did it.

He said, "Every day, for the last ten years, I spent two

hours a day going to this 'field' and planting one 'seed.' I never let the grind of everyday life get in the way and stop me. Now my 'field' produces the most profitable crop in the world."

"What kind of crop is that?" they asked.

"The harvest that I reap is '*The Knowledge of TRUTH and Universal Laws.*' With that, everything you want to happen will fall into place without effort. I used to work very hard and barely made a living, but now I have learned to tap into the Universal Energy and everything just FLOWS naturally. I have a business that runs itself, which provides me with whatever I need. My family relationships are better than ever. I met the most beautiful girl you could ever imagine, we got married and our relationship is one that people dream about.

"I don't understand. All that time we thought you were crazy for doing what you were doing."

"You see, I wasn't planting real seeds in the ground. What I was doing was reading books that taught me the 'SECRETS' of the universe and applying what I read into my life. It's funny, but these 'SECRETS' are not really secret. They are available to everybody who would just 'ask.' A wise man once said, 'Ask and you shall receive.' Well he was right."

"Wow, I wish I had started 'planting those seeds' ten years ago when you did. Now it's probably too late."

"It's never too late. Understand that no matter how old you are, you still have the rest of your life left to learn something new. Remember, *the only seed that does not grow is the one that's never planted.*

> "*Learn as though you are going to live forever....*
> *Live as though you are going to die tomorrow.*"
> - Author Unknown

The Partnership

Way out in the universe, playing amongst the stars, was the one called Spirit. He possessed powers that allowed him to create whatever he wanted the moment he asked for it. Spirit knew the deepest form of love and knew that it was the source of his wonderful powers. Spirit played all day long and enjoyed all the wonderful creations He produced. He particularly enjoyed playing in one specific playground, the one called Earth. This playground posed challenges He could not find in the other playgrounds, which made His playtime there much more satisfying. The most challenging part of this playground was that He was not allowed access unless He had a partner. He could watch everybody playing, but He could do nothing without His partner.

Finding His partner was not as simple as it seemed. His partner was allowed in the playground but couldn't enjoy it to its full potential without his Spirit partner. Now, Spirit knew who His Earth partner was and tried to contact him, but His Earth partner could not hear Him. Even worse, He found that His Earth partner did not remember Him and continued to play by himself, ignoring his Spirit partner and only experiencing a fraction of the enjoyment that was possible.

Spirit waited patiently for His partner to remember Him and ask Him to play. He watched His partner struggle through life, always working so hard that it didn't even seem like playtime anymore. If he only knew how much power his partner had that he could have access to, his life would be greater than he could ever imagine. But in order to access the power of his partner, he first had to remember Him and then he had to ask Him for help. One of the rules of the playground was that the partner could not interfere unless He was asked, and these were rules that were always followed.

One day, the Earth partner found himself in deep trouble. His life was not going the way he thought it was supposed to, in fact, he was now experiencing tremendous pain. He always thought he knew all the answers, but suddenly he realized that he was now out of options. It seems that the pain brought up a hidden memory of his partner and with nowhere else to turn he started to call on his Spirit partner. In an instant, the pain was gone. He couldn't believe it. The Spirit partner said, "There are many things I could do, if you would just give me a chance. What you call a *miracle*, I call 'doing my job.' Please let me do my job. That's all I want to do."

That night, the two partners talked for hours. When they were done, the Earth partner realized that everything they discussed seemed so familiar. It was as if he remembered everything he had forgotten. From that moment on, the two partners would always play together and life for the Earth partner was once again like the games he played when he was a child, but this time his "imaginary" friend was real and whatever he wished for came true.

"All men who have moved the world to better things have received their inspiration from the Spirit within and have always looked to it for instruction."
- Charles Fillmore

Mission of Love

In a far off land, beyond time and space, lived two beings sharing a perfect love. They lived in a land where everything was possible and all their dreams became reality in an instant. *A* and *C* were perfect beings who understood that being together only made them more perfect.

One day, an elder being came to them and brought them news of a troubled land that needed their help. He said the elders had been watching them and that they were chosen to help the people of this troubled land.

"How can we help?" asked *A*.

"By sharing your message," responded the elder.

"What message is that?" inquired *C*.

"Your message of love. We have been watching you for some time now, and it is obvious to us that you understand the TRUE meaning of love. This land that needs your help has forgotten what TRUE LOVE is. We have sent teachers before but the people of this land are still lost. The time is now right for you to teach these people about LOVE."

𝐴 and 𝐶 understood TRUE LOVE meant sharing, not just with each other, but with everyone, so they agreed to take on this mission.

"I must caution you," said the elder. "There are certain things you must be made aware of. In order for you to complete your mission, you will have to go as people from their land; you must be one of them. You will lose all the powers that you have here except one – the power of LOVE."

𝐴 and 𝐶 looked at each other and they both understood that as long as they had the power of LOVE, they would be able to complete their mission.

"One more thing. You will forget everything that you know here, including who you are."

"Will I remember 𝐶?" asked 𝐴.

"No."

"I don't understand. How will we complete our mission?" 𝐶 asked.

"It will become clear. When the time is right, and you both are ready, you will meet. Then your mission will begin. Until then, your time will be spent learning the ways of this new land and their people."

"If I don't remember 𝐶, how will I know her when I meet her?"

"You will be given signs. Have faith in the signs. They will lead you back to your TRUE LOVE."

"What kind of signs?"

"You will know them when you see them. They will appear when you are both ready to understand them. I want to warn you both, though. During the early years, there will be those who appear in your lives that you will think are your TRUE LOVE, but they are not. They will be part of the lesson meant to prepare you."

"But how will we know who is the lesson and who is our TRUE LOVE?"

"The signs never lie. Just be aware of the signs. Be careful, and make sure you read them correctly. If you don't, you can ruin your mission. You will be given signs to show you who is a lesson, and you will be given signs to show you who is your TRUE LOVE. If you know how to read the signs properly, they will be obvious to you. But if you misinterpret them, the mission cannot begin, and the suffering will continue for the people of this land. The mission will begin when you both read the signs properly and have been united. Neither of you can accomplish the mission without the other. I cannot stress enough how important this is. I will give you one clue, though. The eyes are a gateway to the REAL YOU. Look for the hidden messages that come through the eyes."

A and C stared deeply and passionately into each other's eyes to try to remember something that would help identify the other when they met. They embraced, took a deep breath, and then they were off to prepare for their mission...their MISSION OF LOVE.

(TO BE CONTINUED...)

Mission of Love
— Part 2 —
The Preparation

𝒜 and 𝒞 were off to prepare for their Mission of Love. Each was assigned a guide who would help them through the preparation process. They were then led down separate hallways to begin.

The first stop resembled a giant theater. 𝒜 and his guide, Gia, went inside and walked to the center of this grand theater where 𝒜 was directed to step inside the Ring of Destiny. 𝒜's eyes widened in wonder as Gia explained that this was where 𝒜 would make his life selection. Surrounding the Ring of Destiny were screens that would allow 𝒜 to view some of the future events of the possible life choices that were presented. It's as if he was allowed a dress rehearsal before making a final choice. After experiencing all the choices and feeling that he had enough knowledge of all of his options, 𝒜 was ready to make a decision. He felt scenario #3 would provide the perfect opportunity to allow him to get acclimated to the new land, while at the same time provide him with the skills needed to complete his mission. Gia told him that once these skills had been acquired, his memory would be triggered and the wisdom needed in addition to the skills, would start to become clear, and that one could not be used without the other.

Next, it was time for 𝒜 to choose a body that would be most useful for his mission. He knew what skills would be important so he chose a body that would allow easier acclimation to those skills. Then, it was off to the Hall of Recognition where he found C already waiting for him. They embraced and were grateful to be given one last chance to see each other before they left. It was here that they would go over the signs that would allow them to remember one another in the new land. They understood that they would not recognize each other at first, so these signs were extremely important to awaken the hidden memories of the other and the love they shared. They were given many signs, some designed as primary memory triggers and others as backups, in case the primary ones were missed. This part was extremely important because they both understood that the mission could not begin if they did not come together.

𝒜 and C were then led to a small room filled with a beautiful light were it was time to go over final preparation and learn more about the mission. Before leaving, Gia said to 𝒜, "When you are down there, I will always be near you ready to help. You will not be able to see me but know that I'll be with you. I am forbidden from interfering unless you ask, though, so ask and it shall be granted." He then bowed and walked away.

One of the elders, the one called Endar, was waiting inside. Endar had a beautiful voice that seemed to reach deep inside them as he spoke. "You have chosen an important journey, but you must understand a few things first. Know that you are pure and powerful energy and the physical body you have chosen could not handle all of this energy so only a portion will be sent into your body. You will have access to the rest once you have reached a point of remembrance. There will be many ways to access this power; the first one is by shedding the overlays that will be imprinted in the early years of life. These overlays block the connection to your power so they must be cleared. The next way to access this power, the deepest parts of this Power of Love, is by coming together in physical union. 𝒜, you will notice that you will be equipped with a "key" and C, you will be fitted with a "lock." 𝒜, your key will fit other locks and C, your lock will allow different keys but only your key, 𝒜, will be the one that unlocks C's lock to your deepest power. Your key and lock are not to be used foolishly as they can unleash the wrong kind of power so you must be careful. You must purify yourselves of all the lower energies you've accumulated in your early years before you can unlock the gate to "The Corridor of Power." It's through this corridor that the pure power that has been held in reserve will flow to you and give you the abilities needed to fulfill your mission. Without this power, you will be defeated. The opposition is extremely powerful and they will do all they can to prolong their existence."

"Tell us about the opposition," 𝒜 asked.

"I will explain more about them in a moment but first I must explain a few more important things," replied Endar. "Over here, you create what you focus on instantly. In this new land, you will also create what you focus on, but the difference is it will not be instantly. There will be a delay before your thoughts materialize, but know that they will. This delay is the reason the people are not aware of their creative power. You must show them this is so.

One last thing, remember that you will be "in" their land but not "of" their land. You must not get lost in the things of their land or they will keep you from your mission. You will be able to enjoy all the wonderful things that are there for everyone's pleasure, but you must keep them in their proper perspective. I cannot tell you how many beings went down on similar missions only to get lost in the pleasures of the flesh, the senses and the land, and were not able to complete their missions.

OK. Now it's time to tell you about the opposition you'll be facing and how they are controlling the people of this land. Listen closely because, in order to defeat them you must first understand how everything came to be."

(TO BE CONTINUED...)

The story of *A* & *C* will continue in it's own book,
"Mission of Love – A Tale of Hidden Truths & the Power of Love"
- coming 2003 -

— Part 3—

Miracles In Our Lives

As we go through life, we are constantly
surrounded by examples of the Divine. These
stories are a collection of "Miracles" that will get
you in touch with your Inner Spirit and allow you to
feel your connection to the Divine.

The Conversation Begins...

I've always considered myself a good person with a strong belief in God. My idea of God, of course, was one that I learned from my parents as I was growing up. I've always considered my relationship with God like I view my relationship with the President; I know he's there, I respect his authority and his power, but I don't know him personally. I've always felt the same about God; I know He's there, I respect His authority and His power, but I've never felt like I've known Him on a personal level.

I found myself going through a challenge in my life that was painful at times, and I wanted to find a solution, not just to stop the pain but to do the right thing as well. Like many of us would do, I started talking to God, but this time something strange happened...He answered me. I asked for a sign, to tell me what to do and I got one within 30 seconds. Over the next two weeks, this occurred every day. One night, I was walking my dogs and I started talking to God, as I had been doing quite often lately. I was telling Him how for the first time in my life, I felt a real connection to Him; I actually felt that he was my friend. I talked to Him like my friend and He would answer me. I said to Him, "I've really enjoyed these conversations we've been having lately. I'm looking forward to having more *conversations with You.*"

The next day, I was at the bookstore buying a book for my brother and I was at the register paying for the book. I looked over the cashier's shoulder and I noticed a few books on the wall. I asked him to hand me one of them. The name of the book was *"Conversations with God."*

That "Conversation" opened a whole new door for me and changed my life completely. It has now been two years since that conversation and every day has been a "miracle." I now realize that He has always been "talking" to me but I did not know how to listen. The beautiful thing is that He "talks" to everyone; you just have to learn how to listen. When you do, your life will never be the same.

- Andrew Moss

"There is a giant asleep within every man. When the giant awakens, miracles happen"
- Frederick Faust

A Lesson in
Unconditional Acceptance

I am a mother of three and have recently completed my college degree. The last class I had to take was Sociology. The teacher was absolutely inspiring, with the qualities that I wish every human being had been graced with. Her last project of the term was called "Smile." The class was asked to go out and smile at three people and document their reaction. I am a very friendly person and always smile at everyone and say "hello" anyway, so I thought this would be a piece of cake.

Soon after we were assigned the project, my husband, youngest son and I went to McDonalds. We were standing in line, waiting to be served, when all of a sudden, everyone around us began to back away, including my husband. I did not move an inch. An overwhelming feeling of panic welled up inside of me as I turned to see why they had moved. As I turned around, I smelled a horrible "dirty body" smell, and there standing behind me were two poor homeless men. One of them was smiling. His beautiful sky-blue eyes were full of God's light as he searched for acceptance. He said, "Good day" as he counted the few coins he had been clutching. The second man fumbled with his hands as he stood behind his friend. I realized the second man was mentally deficient and the blue-eyed gentleman was his salvation. I held my tears as I stood there with them. The young lady at the counter asked him what they wanted. He said, "Coffee is all, Miss" because that was all they could afford. They just wanted to stay warm and they knew they had to buy something. Then I really felt it, the compulsion was so great I almost reached out and embraced the little man with the blue eyes. That is when I noticed all eyes in the restaurant were set on me, judging my reaction. I smiled and asked the lady behind the counter to give me two more breakfast meals on a separate tray. I then walked around the corner to the table the men had chosen as a resting spot. I put the tray on the table and laid my hand on the blue-eyed gentleman's cold hand. He looked up at me with tears in his eyes and said, "Thank you." I leaned over, began to pat his hand and said, "I did not do this for you. God is here working though me to give you hope." I started to cry as I walked away to join my husband and son. When I sat down, my husband smiled at me and said, "That is why God gave you to me, honey. To give me hope." We held hands for a moment and we knew it was only because of the Grace that we had been given that we were able to give. We are not church-goers but we are believers. That day showed me the pure light of God's sweet love.

I returned to college on the last evening of the class with this story in hand. I turned in my "project" and the instructor read it. She looked up at me and asked, "Can I share this?" I slowly nodded as she got the attention of the class. She began to read, and just then I realized that we, as human beings and being part of God, share this need to heal people and be healed. In my own way, I had touched the people at McDonalds, my husband, son, instructor and every soul that shared the classroom on the last night I spent as a college student. I graduated with one of the biggest lessons I would ever learn...UNCONDITIONAL ACCEPTANCE.

- Contributed Anonymously

"What if I should discover that the poorest of the beggars and the most impudent of offenders are all within me, and that I stand in need of the alms of my own kindness; that I myself am the enemy who must be loved – what then?"

- Carl Jung

A Love Story

They were childhood friends since the third grade and were in love before they knew what love was. It would be almost ten years before they realized it. Maria was a beautiful young girl – the star athlete – and very popular. Paul was an overweight teenager, who could be counted on to always do the right thing. Nobody would have guessed that these two would ever become an "item" ... except Paul. For years, Maria was the only girl he would think of, hoping and praying for the day she would feel the same. They lost touch for a few years. By the time they reconnected Maria had blossomed into a beautiful woman and Paul had grown into a very good-looking man, losing the extra weight he carried as a teenager.

As time went on, they grew closer, until one day they both realized that they shared the same deep feelings of love for one another. They spent as much time as they could together, always working around their college classes and work schedules. They were both very responsible and knew the time would come when there would not be so many distractions. Unfortunately, that proved to be wishful thinking, as pressure from both families kept growing and pulling them apart. One side was pushing marriage; the other was totally against it. Paul did all he could to remain true to his love, while at the same time remaining responsible, trying to complete school and secure a stable job before crossing the "marriage" line.

Alas, the pressure got to be too much and their relationship was over. Paul was devastated by the pain. He accepted a job in Florida, hoping that the pain would remain in New York with the rest of his shattered dreams.

As time went by, Paul grew to enjoy life in Florida, but nothing ever brought about the passion for life that he enjoyed with Maria. From time to time, he played around with the dating scene but it was obvious that something was missing. Meanwhile, Maria got engaged and then married in order to escape the pain she was going through and take control over her own life. She knew that once she was on her own she would be the one in charge of her life's decisions.

When Paul found out about this, he was crushed. They had not spoken since he left New York, but he had always clung to the hope that there was still a chance. Now he was sure there was none. Nine years went by and Paul found himself searching for something in his life, but he did not know what it was. Something was calling him back to New York. He felt that he needed to be there. He knew it was time to return.

I spoke with Paul just before Christmas, and for the first time in years he had passion in his voice. He was excited about a new relationship he was involved in and wanted me to meet her. I was so happy for him, because someone had finally ignited that flame inside him and he could get on with his life. We had arranged to meet for dinner on Christmas Eve. An hour before the dinner, my mother had been questioning when I was going to meet that "right girl." I said, "When God feels we are ready, the right one is presented." When Paul arrived at the restaurant and introduced me to his "love," tears welled up in my eyes as Maria stepped out from behind him. After nine years, God knew they were ready, and presented each other with their one TRUE love.

- Andrew Moss

"The way to love anything is to realize that it might be lost."
- G.K. Chesterton

The Joy of Giving

I remember it like it was yesterday. I was eleven years old and my mom and dad were arguing on Thanksgiving Day. My dad was feeling the pressure of not earning enough money to support our family and was venting his frustrations out on my mother when the doorbell rang. I ran to the door and, to my surprise, there stood a gentleman we did not know holding a Thanksgiving feast someone had sent for my family. I was so happy because I thought this would mean our family could celebrate this beautiful day and stop fighting. I called my dad to the door and eagerly awaited his reaction. My jaw dropped open as he slammed the door in the man's face. "We don't accept charity!" he yelled. I was torn between two feelings; I was crushed that my father would react in such a horrible way to such a beautiful gesture but at the same time I was touched that someone would be kind enough to send such love. I guess that day was too much for my dad to handle because shortly thereafter he left the family and we were left on our own. That day was also a turning point for me because I promised myself that one day I would do the same for another needy family.

I grew up driven by the desire to succeed where my father

had failed. I was not angry at my father; in fact, I had compassion for the way this poor man must have suffered to feel the need to abandon his family.

Fifteen years later I found myself running a successful business when the thought occurred to me that I had come full circle. I was now in a position to help a family that was in the same position as mine was fifteen years earlier. I decided that on Thanksgiving Day, I would bless someone the way we had been blessed, with an anonymous gift of a Thanksgiving feast. I went to the store and purchased all of the trimmings and drove to a family that I knew was in dire need of help. I pretended to be the delivery boy and told them that someone wanted them to have this great meal. I thought to myself, I just wanted to be there to see the expression on their faces; that was all the thanks I needed. The family did not speak any English, but I managed to understand everything they were feeling as I handed them the huge platter of food. The whole family came out and thanked me like I had never been thanked before. They hugged and kissed me, each and every one of them. As I drove off, I looked back and the whole family was standing on the porch, and I could see the mother wipe the tears from her eyes as she waved goodbye to me. I realized that I never felt so good in my whole life as I wiped the tears from my own eyes.

The following year I did the same for two families, the year after that, for four, then eight and finally sixteen. At that point I got my whole company involved. Since that time, it has become an annual tradition to make sure needy people are able to experience what Thanksgiving means.

I have since started my own non-profit foundation, and last year we gave away 125,000 free Thanksgiving dinners. I now look forward to that time of the year when I touch my own spirit, as well as the spirit of others, as I experience the joy of giving on a day that is appropriately named, Thanksgiving.

- *Anthony Robbins (adapted)*

"We make a living by what we get, we make a life by what we give."
- Sir Winston Churchill

We Are Never Alone

Last summer, my family had a spiritual experience that had a lasting and profound impact on us; one we feel must be shared. It's a message of love, of regaining perspective and renewing priorities.

On July 22nd, I was en route to Washington D.C. for a business trip. It was very ordinary until we landed in Denver for a plane change. As I collected my belongings from the overhead bin an announcement was made for Mr. Lloyd Glenn to see the Customer Service Rep immediately. At this point I knew something was wrong and my heart sunk. A solemn-faced young man came toward me and said, "Mr. Glenn, there is an emergency at your home." My heart was now pounding but the will to be calm took over. I called the number I was given and was put through to the trauma center. I learned that my three-year old son had been trapped underneath the automatic garage door for several minutes, and that when my wife had found him, he was dead. By the time I called,

Brian was revived and they believed he would live but they did not know how much damage had been done to his brain or his heart.

I arrived at the hospital six hours after the garage door had come down. When I walked into the intensive care unit nothing could have prepared me for what I saw. There was my little son lying so still, hooked up to a respirator, with tubes and monitors everywhere. Finally, the next day, our son regained consciousness and sat up uttering the most beautiful words I had ever heard. He said, "Daddy, hold me," and he reached for me with his little arms. The next day he was diagnosed as having no neurological or physical deficits, and the story of his miraculous survival spread throughout the hospital. As we took Brian home, we felt a unique reverence for life as we experienced the love of our Heavenly Father that comes to those who brush death so closely. In the days that followed there was a special spirit about our home. All of us grew closer as a family. Life took on a less stressful pace. We felt deeply blessed.

The story is not over. Almost a month later, Brian awoke from his afternoon nap and said, "Sit down mommy. I have something to tell you." At this time in his life, Brian usually spoke in small phrases so to utter this large a sentence was a surprise to my wife. She sat down with him and he started his remarkable story. "Do you remember when I got stuck under the garage door? Well, it was so heavy and hurt really bad. I called to you, but you couldn't hear me. I started to cry and then the birdies came." "The birdies?" my wife asked. "Yes, the birdies took care of me. One of the birdies came and got you. She came to tell you I got stuck under the door." My wife realized that a three-year old had no concept of death and spirits, so he was referring to the beings that came to him as "birdies." "What did they look like?" she asked. "They were so beautiful, dressed in white," he answered. "Did they say anything?" "Yes, they told me the baby would be alright. You came to the garage and told the baby to stay and not leave." My wife nearly collapsed, for when she saw him and thought he was dead, she whispered, "Don't leave us Brian; please stay if you can." She realized that his spirit had left his body and was looking down from above. "Then what happened?" she asked. "We went on a trip far, far away. The birdies said I had to come back and tell everybody about them. The birdies are always with us, but we don't see them because we look with our eyes and we don't hear them because we listen with our ears. But they are always there. You can only see them in here (he put his hand over his heart). They whisper the things to help us do what is right because they love us so much. I have a plan, mommy. You have a plan, daddy has a plan, everybody has a plan. We must all live our plan and keep our promises." In the weeks that followed, he often repeated the story and it always remained the same. It never ceased to amaze us how he could tell such detail and speak beyond his ability when he spoke of his "birdies." Needless to say, we have not been the same ever since that day and I pray we never will.

– Contributed Anonymously

"Be bold – and mighty forces will come to your aid."
- Basil King

The Old Fisherman

Our house was directly across the street from the clinic entrance to John Hopkins Hospital. We lived downstairs and rented the upstairs rooms to outpatients at the clinic. One summer evening, as I was fixing supper there was a knock at the door. I opened it to see a truly awful looking man. "Why, he's hardly taller than my eight-year old," I thought as I stared at the stooped, shriveled body. But the appalling thing was his face – lopsided from swelling, red and raw. Yet his voice was pleasant as he said, "Good evening. I've come to see if you've a room for just one night. I came for treatment this morning from the eastern shore, and there's no bus 'til morning." He told me he'd been hunting for a room since noon but with no success, no one seemed to have a room. "I guess it's my face. I know it looks terrible, but my doctor says with a few more treatments…" For a moment I hesitated, but his next words convinced me: "I could sleep in this rocking chair on the porch. My bus leaves early in the morning." I told him we would find him a bed, but to rest on the porch. I went inside and finished getting supper. When we were ready, I asked the old man if he would join us. "No thank you, I have plenty." And he held up a brown paper bag.

After dinner, I went out on the porch to talk with him a few minutes. It didn't take long to see that this old man had an oversized heart crowded into that tiny body. He told me he fished for a living to support his daughter, her five children and her husband, who was hopelessly crippled from a back injury. He didn't tell it by way of complaint; in fact, every other sentence was prefaced with a thanks to God for a blessing. He was grateful that no pain accompanied his disease, which was apparently a form of skin cancer. He thanked God for giving him the strength to keep going.

At bedtime, we put a camp cot in the children's room for him. When I got up in the morning, the bed linens were neatly folded and the little man was out on the porch. He refused breakfast, but just before he left for his bus, haltingly, as if asking a great favor, he said, "Could I please come back and stay the next time I have a treatment? I won't put you out a bit. I can sleep in a chair." I told him he was welcome to come again.

On his next trip he arrived a little after seven in the morning. As a gift he brought a big fish and a quart of the largest oysters I had ever seen. He said he had shucked them that morning before he left so that they'd be nice and fresh. I knew his bus left at 4:00 a.m. and I wondered what time he had to get up in order to do this for us.

In the years he came to stay overnight with us there was never a time that he did not bring us fish or oysters or vegetables from his garden. Other times we received packages in the mail, always by special delivery. Knowing that he must walk three miles to mail these, and knowing how little money he had made the gifts doubly precious. When I received these little remembrances, I often thought of a comment our neighbor made after he left that first morning. "Did you keep that awful looking man last night? I turned him away! You can lose roomers by putting up such people!" Maybe we did lose roomers once or twice, but if they could have known him, perhaps their illnesses would have been easier to bear. I know our family always will be grateful to have known him; from him we learned what it was to accept the bad without complaint and the good with gratitude to God.

Recently I was visiting a friend who has a greenhouse. As she showed me her flowers, we came to the most beautiful one of all. But to my great surprise, it was growing in an old dented, rusty bucket. I thought to myself, "If this were my plant, I'd put it in the loveliest container I had." My friend changed my mind. "I ran short of pots," she explained, "and knowing how beautiful this one would be, I thought it wouldn't mind starting out in this old pail. It's just for a little while, 'til I can put it out into the garden." She must have wondered why I laughed so delightedly, but I was imagining just such a scene in heaven. "Here's an especially beautiful one," God might have said when he came to the soul of the sweet old fisherman. "He won't mind starting in this small body." All this happened long ago and now, in God's garden, how tall this lovely soul must stand. The Lord does not look at the things man looks at. Man looks at the outward appearance, but the Lord looks at the heart.

- Contributed Anonymously

"Be kind, for everyone you meet is fighting a hard battle."
- Plato

A Sandpiper to Bring You Joy

She was six years old when I first met her on the beach near where I live. I drive to this beach whenever the world begins to close in on me. She was building a sandcastle and looked up, her eyes as blue as the sea. "Hello," she said. I answered with a nod, not really in the mood to bother with a small child. "I'm building," she said. "I see that. What is it?" I asked, not caring. "Oh, I don't know, I just like the feel of sand." That sounds good, I thought, and slipped off my shoes. A sandpiper glided by. "That's a joy," the child said. "It's a what?" "It's a joy. My mama says sandpipers come to bring us joy." The bird went gliding down the beach. "Goodbye joy," I muttered to myself, "hello pain," and turned to walk on. I was depressed; my life seemed completely out of balance. "What's your name?" She wouldn't give up. "Robert," I answered, "Robert Peterson." "Mine's Wendy... I'm six." "Hi Wendy." She giggled. "You're funny," she said. In spite of my gloom I laughed too and walked on. Her musical giggle followed me. "Come again, Mr. P.," she called. "We'll have another happy day."

The days and weeks that followed belonged to others: a group of unruly Boy Scouts, PTA meetings and an ailing mother. The sun was shining one morning as I said to myself, "I need a sandpiper," and gathered up my coat. The ever-changing balm of the seashore awaited me. The breeze was chilly but I strode along trying to recapture the serenity I needed. I had forgotten the child and was startled when she appeared. "Hello, Mr. P.," she said. "Do you want to play?" "What do you have in mind?" I asked, with a twinge of annoyance. "I don't know." "How about charades?" I asked sarcastically. The tinkling laughter burst forth again. "I don't know what that is." "Then let's just walk." Looking at her, I noticed the delicate fairness of her face. "Where do you live?" I asked. "Over there." She pointed toward a row of summer cottages. Strange, I thought, in winter. "Where do you go to school?" "I don't go to school. Mommy says we're on vacation." She chattered little girl talk as we strolled up the beach, but my mind was on other things. When I left for home, Wendy said it had been a happy day. Feeling surprisingly better, I smiled at her and agreed.

Three weeks later, I rushed to my beach in a state of near panic. I was in no mood to even greet Wendy. I thought I saw her mother on the porch and felt like demanding she keep her child at home. "Look, if you don't mind," I said crossly when Wendy caught up with me, "I'd rather be alone today." She seemed unusually pale and out of breath. "Why?" she asked. I turned to her and shouted, "Because my mother died!" and I thought, my God, why was I saying this to a little child? "Oh," she said quietly, "then this is a bad day." "Yes," I said, "and yesterday and the day before and...oh, go away!" "Did it hurt?" she inquired. "Did what hurt?" I was exasperated with her. "When she died?" "Of course it hurt!!" I snapped, misunderstanding, wrapped up in myself. I strode off.

A month or so after that, when I next went to the beach, she wasn't there. Feeling guilty, ashamed and admitting to myself I missed her, I went up to the cottage after my walk and knocked at the door. A drawn looking young woman opened the door. "Hello," I said, "I'm Robert Peterson. I missed your little girl today and wondered where she was." "Oh yes, Mr. Peterson, please come in. Wendy spoke of you so much. I'm afraid I allowed her to bother you. If she was a nuisance, please accept my apologies." "Not at all, she's a delightful child," I said, suddenly realizing that I meant it. "Where is she?" "Wendy died last week. She had leukemia. Maybe she didn't tell you. She loved this beach; so when she asked me to come, we couldn't say no. She seemed so much better here and had a lot of what she called happy days. But the last few weeks, she declined rapidly..." her voice faltered. "She left something for you." She handed me a smeared envelope, with Mr. P. on it. Inside was a crayon drawing of a yellow beach, a blue sea, and a brown bird. Underneath was written: "A Sandpiper to bring you Joy." Tears welled up in my eyes, and a heart that had almost forgotten how to open, opened wide. I took Wendy's mother in my arms. "I'm so sorry," I muttered over and over, and we wept together. The precious little picture is framed now and hangs in my study. Six words – one for each year of her life – that speak to me of harmony, courage and undemanding love. A gift from a child with sea-blue eyes and hair the color of sand, who taught me the gift of love.

- Contributed Anonymously

"Beginning today, treat everyone you meet as if they were going to be dead by midnight. Extend to them all the care, kindness and understanding you can muster, and do with no thought of any reward. Your life will never be the same again."
- Og Mandino

"Keep Your Fork"

There was a woman who had been diagnosed with a terminal illness and had been given three months to live. As she was getting her things "in order" she contacted her pastor and had him come to her house to discuss certain aspects of her final wishes. She told him which songs she wanted sung at the service, what scriptures she would like read, and what outfit she wanted to be buried in. The woman also requested to be buried with her favorite Bible.

Everything was in order and the pastor was preparing to leave when the woman suddenly remembered something very important to her.

"There's one more thing," she said excitedly.

"What's that?" came the pastor's reply.

"This is very important," the woman continued... "I want to be buried with my fork in my right hand."

The pastor stood looking at the woman, not knowing quite what to say.

"That surprises you, doesn't it?" the woman asked.

"Well, to be honest, I'm puzzled by the request," said the pastor.

The woman explained, "In all my years of attending church socials and potluck dinners, I always remember that when the dishes of the main course were being cleared, someone would inevitably lean over and say, "Keep your fork." It was my favorite part because I knew that something better was coming... like velvety chocolate cake or deep-dish apple pie. Something wonderful, and with substance! So, I just want people to see me there in that casket with a fork in my hand and I want them to wonder, 'What's with the fork?' Then I want you to tell them: 'Keep your fork. The best is yet to come!'"

The pastor's eyes welled up with tears of joy as he hugged the woman goodbye. He knew this would be one of the last times he would see her before her death. But he also knew that the woman had a better grasp of heaven than he did. She KNEW that something better was coming.

At the funeral, people were walking by the woman's casket and they saw the pretty dress she was wearing and her favorite Bible and the fork placed in her right hand. Over and over the pastor heard the question, "What's with the fork?" And over and over he smiled. During his message, the pastor told the people of the conversation he had with the woman shortly before she died. He also told them about the fork and what it symbolized to her. The pastor told the people how he could not stop thinking about the fork and told them that they probably would not be able to stop thinking about it either. He was right. So the next time you reach down for your fork, let it remind you, oh so gently, that the best is yet to come...!

- Contributed Anonymously

"Don't make the excuse that man is only human. With all the force of the truth that is in us, we say, we know that man is divine."
- White Eagle

Attitude Is Everything

Michael is the kind of guy you love to hate. He is always in a good mood and has something positive to say. When someone would ask him how he was doing, he would reply, "If I were any better, I'd be twins!" He was a natural motivator. If an employee was having a bad day, Michael was there telling the employee how to look on the positive side of the situation. Seeing this style really made me curious, so one day I went up to Michael and asked him, "I don't get it. You can't be positive all the time. How do you do it?"

Michael replied, "Each morning I wake up and say to myself, 'Mike, you have two choices today. You can choose to be in a good mood or you can choose to be in a bad mood.' I choose to be in a good mood. Each time something bad happens, I can choose to be a victim or choose to learn from it. I choose to learn from it. Every time someone comes to me complaining, I can choose to accept their complaining or I can point out the positive side of life. I choose the positive side of life."

"Yeah, right. It isn't that easy," I protested.

"Yes it is," Michael said. "Life is all about choices. When you cut away all the junk, every situation is a choice. YOU choose how you react to situations. YOU choose how people will affect your mood. YOU choose to be in a good mood or a bad mood. The bottom line is: It's your choice how you live life."

I reflected on what Michael said. Soon thereafter, I left the tower industry to start my own business. We lost touch, but I often thought about him when I made a choice about life instead of reacting to it.

Several years later, I heard Michael was involved in a serious accident, falling some 60 feet from a communications tower. After 18 hours of surgery and weeks of intensive care, Michael was released from the hospital with rods inserted in his back. I saw Michael about six months after the accident. When I asked him how he was, he replied, "If I were any better, I'd be twins. Wanna see my scars?"

I declined to see his wounds, but did ask him what had gone through his mind as the accident happened.

"The first thing that went through my mind was the well being of my soon-to-be-born daughter," Michael replied. "Then, as I lay on the ground, I remembered I had two choices: I could choose to live or I could choose to die. I chose to live."

"Weren't you scared? Did you lose consciousness?" I asked.

Michael continued, "The paramedics were great. They kept telling me I was going to be fine. But when they wheeled me into the ER and I saw the expressions on the faces of the doctors and nurses, I got really scared. In their eyes, I read, 'He's a dead man.' I knew I needed to take action."

"What did you do?" I asked.

"Well, there was this big, burly nurse shouting questions at me," said Michael. "She asked me if I was allergic to anything. 'Yes,' I said. The doctors and nurses stopped working as they waited for my reply. I took a deep breath and yelled, 'Gravity!' Over their laughter, I told them, 'I am choosing to live. Operate on me as if I'm alive, not dead.'"

Michael lived because of his amazing attitude. I learned

from him that every day we have a choice to live fully. Attitude is everything.

- Contributed Anonymously

"Your life is determined not so much by what life brings you as by the attitude you bring to life; not so much by what happens to you as by the way your mind looks at what happens."
- Lewis L. Dunnington

Footprints in the Sand

When my husband and I were living in California pursuing my acting career, we were the only ones we had, as our entire family lived on the East Coast. Both of us were working meaningless temporary jobs to make ends meet. In addition to my temp job, I was working as a stagehand in a production at the local playhouse and was passed over to understudy for one of the actresses who had to leave the play. And, to top it off, the pregnancy test I took that week came out negative; a huge letdown for me and my husband who were eager to start a family.

I was having an extremely stressful day in this unusually hectic week. I was doing double work for a co-worker on vacation. This particular day I was having was going so badly. Something in me was telling me to leave work early and take a walk on the beach. I told my boss I needed to leave early and since he realized I was working extra hard that week, he agreed that it would be a good idea. I drove home, got changed and stepped outside to take my walk. We had the good fortune to live right on the beach; in fact, the sand began literally right outside our apartment building.

I immediately started to feel recharged but I still felt that I had so many unanswered questions on my mind. I felt lonely because I was missing my family back East, I was disgruntled with the fact that I was working as a stagehand on the play rather than acting in it and I was questioning why my husband and I had moved so far away from family and friends. Feeling unfocused and confused, I felt like I wasn't contributing anything worthwhile to mankind and that God had forgotten about me.

I continued walking as the waves gently tumbled to the sand. I began talking to God. I asked Him the questions that were concerning me. "Why was I here, so far away from my family? What's happening with my career? How come I'm not acting?" and most importantly, "What am I supposed to be doing with my life? Please show me what to do." At that moment, I looked down and saw two tiny footprints in the sand. It was then that I realized that I was indeed pregnant and that my mission, for the present time, was to take care of the baby growing inside of me. An absolute calm took over me and I innately felt the answers to all the questions that were bothering me. All of the trivial matters that I was worrying about no longer seemed important. I now felt the focus that I was lacking and knew that nothing was as important as bringing this child into the world. It was the sign that I so desperately needed and I allowed myself to see.

From that moment on, I had a new attitude on life. I knew that I was exactly where I needed to be at that time. I felt so much better after this revelation that I cried with relief and joy. I thanked God for showing me this sign and allowing me to understand the message. I knew that I would be taken care of and that God had not forgotten about me.

After that day, in two weeks time, a complete change had occurred in my life. On Christmas Eve, I took another pregnancy test and it was positive. I was six weeks pregnant and I had left my extremely stressful temp job and found a part-time job in a relaxed atmosphere. The play I was working on had ended and then I was offered an acting role in "Cinderella" for the Children's Theater at the Playhouse. My husband and I were ecstatic over the successful conception of our baby and couldn't wait to bring her into the world. Everything that I felt at the moment I saw the sign had come to fruition and my quality of life changed dramatically.

Our daughter was born in August and completely changed my life in ways that I never imagined she would. She taught me to live completely in each moment and not to worry about the unknown situations that we have no control over. She taught me all of this without saying a word.

– *Kathy Fassbender*

"Real joy comes not from ease or riches or from praise of men, but from doing something worthwhile."
- Sir Wifred Grenfell

The Miracle of a Brother's Song

Like any good mother, when Karen found out that another baby was on the way, she did what she could to help her 3-year-old son, Michael, prepare for a new sibling. They found out that the new baby was going to be a girl and, day after day, night after night, Michael sang to his little sister in Mommy's tummy. He was building a bond of love with his little sister before he even met her.

The pregnancy progressed normally for Karen and, in time, the labor pains came. Soon it was every five minutes, every three, then every minute. But serious complications arose during delivery and Karen found herself in hours of labor. Would a C-section be required? Finally, after a long struggle, Michael's little sister was born but she was in very serious condition. With a siren howling in the night, the ambulance rushed the infant to the neonatal intensive care unit at St. Mary's Hospital.

The days inched by. The little girl got worse. The pediatric specialist regretfully had to tell the parents, "There is very little hope. Be prepared for the worst." Karen and her husband contacted a local cemetery about a burial plot. They had fixed up a special room in their home for the new baby, but now they found themselves having to plan for a funeral. Michael, however, kept begging his parents to let him see his sister. "I want to sing to her," he kept saying.

Week two in intensive care looked as if a funeral would come before the week was over. Michael kept nagging about singing to his sister, but kids are never allowed in the Intensive Care Unit. Karen made up her mind, though. She would take Michael, whether they liked it or not! If he didn't see his sister right then, he may never see her alive. She dressed him in an oversized scrub suit and marched him into ICU. He looked like a walking laundry basket, but the head nurse recognized him as a child and bellowed, "Get that kid out of here now! NO children are allowed!" The mother rose strong in Karen and the usually mild-mannered lady glared steel-eyed right into the head nurse's face, her lips a firm line. "He is not leaving until he sings to his sister!" Karen towed Michael to his sister's bedside. He gazed at the tiny infant losing the battle to live. After a moment, he began to sing. In the pure hearted voice of a 3-year-old, Michael sang: *"You are my sunshine, my only sunshine; you make me happy when skies are gray."* Instantly, the baby girl seemed to respond. Her pulse rate began to calm down and become steady. "Keep on singing, Michael," encouraged Karen with tears in her eyes. *"You never know, dear, how much I love you. Please don't take my sunshine away."*

As Michael sang to his sister, the baby's ragged, strained breathing became as smooth as a kitten's purr. "Keep on singing, sweetheart!" *"The other night, dear, as I lay sleeping, I dreamed I held you in my arms..."* Michael's little sister began to relax as rest, healing rest, seemed to sweep over her. "Keep on singing, Michael." Tears had now conquered the face of the bossy head nurse. Karen glowed. *"You are my sunshine, my only sunshine. Please don't take my sunshine away."*

The next day, the very next day, the little girl was well enough to go home! Woman's Day Magazine called it "The

Miracle of a Brother's Song." The medical staff just called it a miracle. Karen called it a miracle of God's love!

Never give up on the people you love. Love is so incredibly powerful.

– Contributed Anonymously

"There is no difficulty that enough love will not conquer; no disease that enough love will not heal; no door that enough love will not open; no gulf that enough love will not bridge, no wall that enough love will not throw down; no sin that enough love will not redeem."
- Emmet Fox

A Christmas Story

It's just a small, white envelope stuck among the branches of our Christmas tree. No name, no ID, no inscription. It has peeked through the branches of our tree for the past 10 years.

It all began because my husband, Mike, hated Christmas – oh, not the true meaning of Christmas, but the commercial aspects of it—overspending, the frantic running around for the last minute gift. Knowing he felt this way, I decided one year to bypass the usual shirts, sweaters, ties, etc. I reached for something special just for Mike. The inspiration came in an unusual way. Our son Kevin, who was 12 that year, was wrestling at the junior level at the school he attended; and shortly before Christmas, there was a non-league match against a team sponsored by an inner-city church, mostly black. These youngsters, dressed in sneakers so ragged that shoestrings seemed to be the only thing holding them together, presented a sharp contrast to our boys in their spiffy blue and gold uniforms and sparkling new wrestling shoes. As the match began, I was alarmed to see that the other team was wrestling without headgear, a kind of light helmet designed to protect a wrestler's ears. It was a luxury the ragtag team obviously could not afford. Well, we ended up walloping them. We took every weight class. And as each of their boys got up from the mat, he swaggered around in tatters with false bravado, a kind of street pride that couldn't acknowledge defeat. Mike, seated beside me, shook his head sadly. "I wish one of them could have won," he said. "They have a lot of potential, but losing like this could take the heart right out of them." Mike loved kids—all kids—and he knew them, having coached little league football, baseball and lacrosse. That's when the idea for his present came.

That afternoon, I went to the local sporting goods store and bought an assortment of wrestling headgear and shoes and sent them anonymously to the inner-city church. On Christmas Eve, I placed the envelope on the tree, the note inside telling Mike what I had done and that this was his gift from me. His smile was the brightest thing about Christmas that year and in succeeding years. For each Christmas, I followed the tradition—one year sending a group of mentally handicapped youngsters to a hockey game, another year a check to a pair of elderly brothers whose home had burned to the ground the week before Christmas, and on and on. The envelope became the highlight of our Christmas. It was always the last thing opened on Christmas morning and our children, ignoring their new toys, would stand with wide-eyed anticipation as their dad lifted the envelope from the tree to reveal its contents. As the children grew, the toys gave way to more practical presents, but the envelope never lost its allure.

The story doesn't end there. You see, we lost Mike last year due to dreaded cancer. When Christmas rolled around, I was still so wrapped in grief that I barely got the tree up. But Christmas Eve found me placing an envelope on the tree, and in the morning, it was joined by three more. Each of our children, unbeknownst to the others, had placed an envelope on the tree for their dad. The tradition has grown and someday will expand even further with our grandchildren standing around the tree with wide-eyed anticipation watching as their fathers take down the envelope. Mike's spirit, like the Christmas spirit, will always be with us.

- Contributed Anonymously

"You have not lived a perfect day, unless you have done something for someone who will never be able to repay you.
- Ruth Smeltzer

The True Test

John Blanchard stood up from the bench straightening his Army uniform, and studied the crowd of people making their way through Grand Central Station. He looked for the girl whose heart he knew but whose face he didn't, the girl with the rose.

His interest in her had begun thirteen months before in a Florida library. Taking a book off the shelf, he found himself intrigued, not with the words of the book, but with the notes penciled in the margin. The soft handwriting reflected a thoughtful soul and insightful mind. In the front of the book, he discovered the previous owner's name, Miss Hollis Maynell. With time and effort he located her address. She lived in New York City.

He wrote her a letter introducing himself and inviting her to correspond. The next day he was shipped overseas for service in World War II. During the next year and one month, the two grew to know each other through the mail. Each letter was a seed falling on a fertile heart. A romance was budding. John requested a photograph, but she refused. She felt that if he really cared, it wouldn't matter what she looked like. When the day finally came for him to return from Europe, they scheduled their first meeting for 7:00 PM at Grand Central Station in New York. "You'll recognize me," she wrote, "by the red rose I'll be wearing on my lapel." So at 7:00 he was in the station looking for a girl whose heart he loved, but whose face he'd never seen.

I'll let Mr. Blanchard tell you what happened: a young woman was coming toward me, her figure long and slim. Her blond hair lay back in curls from her delicate ears; her eyes were blue as flowers. Her lips and chin had a gentle firmness, and in her pale green suit she was like springtime come alive. I started toward her, entirely forgetting to notice that she was not wearing a rose. As I moved, a small, provocative smile curved her lips. "Going my way, sailor?" she murmured. Almost uncontrollably, I made one step closer to her, and then I saw Hollis Maynell. She was standing almost directly behind the girl. A woman well past forty, she had graying hair tucked under a worn hat. She was more than plump, her thick-ankled feet thrust into low-heeled shoes. The girl in the green suit was walking quickly away. I felt as though I was split in two, so keen was my desire to follow her, and yet so deep was my longing for the woman whose spirit had truly companioned me and upheld my own. And there she stood. Her pale, plump face was gentle and sensible; her gray eyes had a warm and kindly twinkle. I did not hesitate. My fingers gripped the small worn blue leather copy of the book that was to identify me to her.

This would not be love, but it would be something precious, something perhaps even better than love, a friendship for which I had been and must ever be grateful. I squared my shoulders and saluted and held out the book to the woman, even though while I spoke, I felt choked by the bitterness of my disappointment.

"I'm John Blanchard, and you must be Miss Maynell. I'm so glad you could meet me; may I take you to dinner?" The woman's face broadened into a tolerant smile. "I don't know what this is about son," she answered, "but the young lady in the green suit who just went by, she begged me to wear this rose on my coat. And she said if you were to ask me to dinner, I should tell you that she is waiting for you in the big restaurant across the street. She said it was some kind of test!"

It's not difficult to understand Miss Maynell's wisdom. The true nature of a heart is seen in its response to the unattractive. "Tell me whom you love," Houssaye wrote, "and I will tell you who you are."

- Contributed Anonymously

"The beginning of love is to let those we love be perfectly themselves, and not to twist them to fit our own image. Otherwise we love only the reflection of ourselves we find in them."
- Thomas Merton

The Father's Eyes

A certain teenager lived alone with his father, and the two of them had a very special relationship. Even though the son was always on the bench, his father was always in the stands cheering. He never missed a game. This young man was still the smallest of the class when he entered high school. His father continued to encourage him but also made it very clear that he did not have to play football if he didn't want to. But the young man loved football and decided to hang in there. He was determined to try his best at every practice, and perhaps he would get to play when he became a senior. All through high school he never missed a practice or a game, but remained a bench warmer for all four years. His faithful father was in the stands for every game, always with words of encouragement for him.

When the young man went to college, he decided to try out for the football team as a "walk-on." Everyone was sure he could never make the cut, but he did. The coach admitted that he kept him on the roster because he always put his heart and soul into every practice and, at the same time, provided the other members with the spirit and hustle they badly needed. The news that he survived the cut thrilled him so much that he rushed to the nearest phone and called his father. His father shared his excitement and was sent season tickets for all the college games. This persistent young athlete never missed practice during his four years at college, but he never got to play in the game.

It was the end of his senior football season, and as he trotted onto the practice field shortly before the big play-off game, the coach met him with a telegram. The young man read the telegram and he became deathly silent. Swallowing hard, he mumbled to the coach, "My father died this morning. Is it all right if I miss practice today?" The coach put his arm around his shoulder and said, "Take the rest of the week off, son. And don't even plan to come back to the game on Saturday."

Then Saturday arrived, and the game was not going well. In the third quarter, when the team was ten points behind, a silent young man quietly slipped into the empty locker room and put on his football gear. As he ran onto the sidelines, the coach and his players were astounded to see their faithful teammate back so soon.

"Coach, please let me play. I've just got to play today," said the young man.

The coach pretended not to hear him. There was no way he wanted his worst player in this close play-off game. But the young man persisted, and finally feeling sorry for the kid, the coach gave in. "All right," he said. "You can go in."

Before long, the coach, the players and everyone in the stands could not believe their eyes. This little unknown, who had never played before, was doing everything right. The opposing team could not stop him. He ran, he passed, he blocked and tackled like a star. His team began to triumph. The score was soon tied. In the closing seconds of the game, this kid intercepted a pass and ran all the way for the winning touchdown. The fans broke loose. His teammates hoisted him onto their shoulders. Such cheering you've never heard!

Finally, after the stands had emptied and the team had showered and left the locker room, the coach noticed the young man was sitting quietly in the corner all alone. The coach came to him and said, "Kid, I can't believe it. You were fantastic! Tell me, what got into you? How did you do it?"

He looked at the coach, with tears in his eyes, and said, "Well, you know my dad died, but did you know that my dad was blind?" The young man swallowed hard and forced a smile. "Dad came to all my games, but today was the first time he could see me play, and I wanted to show him I could do it."

- Contributed Anonymously

"If we did all the things we are capable of doing, we would literally astonish ourselves."
- Thomas Edison

The Best Teacher
He Ever Had

There was a story many years ago of an elementary school teacher. Her name was Mrs. Thompson. And as she stood in front of her fifth grade class on the very first day of school, she told the children a lie. Like most teachers, she looked at her students and said that she loved them all the same. But that was impossible, because in the first row, slumped in his seat, was a little boy named Teddy Stoddard. Mrs. Thompson had watched Teddy the year before and noticed that he didn't play well with the other children, that his clothes were messy and that he constantly needed a bath. And Teddy could be unpleasant. It got to the point where Mrs. Thompson would actually take delight in marking his papers with a broad red pen, making bold X's and then putting a big "F" at the top of his papers.

At the school where Mrs. Thompson taught, she was required to review each child's past records and she put Teddy's off until last. However, when she reviewed his file, she was in for a surprise. Teddy's first grade teacher wrote, "Teddy is a bright child with a ready laugh. He does his work neatly and has good manners...he is a joy to be around." His second grade teacher wrote, "Teddy is an excellent student, well liked by his classmates, but he is troubled because his mother has a terminal illness and life at home must be a struggle." His third grade teacher wrote, "His mother's death has been so hard on him. He tries to do his best but his father doesn't show him much interest and his home life will soon affect him if some steps aren't taken." Teddy's fourth grade teacher wrote, "Teddy is withdrawn and doesn't show much interest in school. He doesn't have many friends and sometimes sleeps in class."

By now, Mrs. Thompson realized the problem and she was ashamed of herself. She felt even worse when her students brought her Christmas presents, wrapped in beautiful ribbons and bright paper, except for Teddy's. His present was clumsily wrapped in the heavy, brown paper that he got from a grocery bag. Mrs. Thompson took pains to open it in the middle of the other presents. Some of the children started to laugh when she found a rhinestone bracelet with some of the stones missing, and a bottle that was one quarter full of perfume. But she stifled the children's laughter when she exclaimed how pretty the bracelet was, putting it on, and dabbing some perfume on her wrist.

Teddy stayed after school that day just long enough to say, "Mrs. Thompson, today you smelled just like my Mom used to." After the children left she cried for at least an hour. On that very day, she quit teaching reading and writing and arithmetic. Instead, she began to teach children.

Mrs. Thompson paid particular attention to Teddy. As she worked with him, his mind seemed to come alive. The more she encouraged him, the faster he responded. By the end of the year, Teddy had become one of the smartest children in the class and, despite her lie that she would love all the children the same, Teddy became one of her teacher's pets. A year later she found a note under her door from Teddy, telling her that she was still the best teacher he ever had in his whole life.

Six years went by before she got another note from Teddy. He then wrote that he had finished high school, third in his class, and she was still the best teacher he ever had in his whole life. Four years after that, she got another letter, saying that while things had been tough at times, he'd stayed in school, had stuck with it, and would soon graduate from college with the highest of honors. He assured Mrs. Thompson that she was still the best teacher he had in his whole life. Then four more years passed by and yet another letter came. This time he explained that after he got his bachelor's degree, he decided to go a little further. The letter explained that she was still the best teacher he ever had. But now his name was a little longer. The letter was signed Theodore F. Stoddard, M.D.

The story doesn't end there. You see, there was yet another letter that spring. Teddy said he'd met this girl and that he was going to be married. He explained that his father had died a couple of years ago and he was wondering if Mrs. Thompson might agree to sit in the place at the wedding that was usually reserved for the mother of the groom. Of course, Mrs. Thompson did. And guess what? She wore that bracelet, the one with the several rhinestones missing. And she made sure she was wearing the perfume that Teddy remembered his mother wearing on their last Christmas together. They hugged each other and Dr. Stoddard whispered in Mrs. Thompson's ear, "Thank you for believing in me. Thank you so much for making me feel important and showing me that I could make a difference."

Mrs. Thompson, with tears in her eyes, whispered back. She said, "Teddy, you have it all wrong. You were the one who taught me that I could make a difference. I didn't know how to teach until I met you."

- Contributed Anonymously

"It is one of the most beautiful compensations of life that no man can sincerely try to help another without helping himself."
- Ralph Waldo Emerson

The Power of Prayer

Doug Coe, who is a remarkable man of faith, told this story about his friend, Bob Hunter. One day when Bob was searching to understand his own faith and what it all meant, he asked Doug, "Do you really believe what the Bible says about moving mountains when we pray?"

Doug thought about it and answered, "Sure."

Bob was rather incredulous and asked him, "Do you mean to say that you believe that if I prayed for a mountain to move, it would move?"

Doug thought for awhile and said, "Let me put it this way. I not only believe it but I will make you a bet. A $500 bet. Bob, what do you know about Africa?"

"Nothing."

"Then here's the bet. I want you to pray for 45 days, 'God help Africa.' You can't miss a single day. And that's all you have to pray: 'God help Africa.' At the end of 45 days, you be the judge on whether any mountains have moved. If you think a mountain has moved, you pay me $500. If not, you just tell me and I'll pay you $500, no questions asked."

Bob, being an astute businessman, rather liked the odds. He accepted the bet. And he began to pray daily, "God help Africa."

A few days later, Bob was attending a formal dinner and sat next to an elderly lady. In the course of the conversation, he found out that she lived in Uganda and ran an orphanage there. Bob asked her a number of questions about Uganda and Africa. After a while, she asked him why he was so interested in Africa. Bob responded, with some embarrassment, "You'll never believe this, but I made a bet with a good friend," and proceeded to tell her about the bet. By the end of the evening, she invited him to return to Uganda with her to visit the orphanage. Bob accepted the invitation. When he visited the orphanage in Uganda, his heart was touched by the orphans. After coming back home, he got a few friends together and bought a load of toys and clothes and sent them to Uganda.

The following week, he got a phone call from the woman. "Mr. Hunter, the children are so grateful for what you did. They would love if you could come again so they can make a special presentation to you to show their appreciation. Can you come?"

Bob accepted the invitation and was off to Uganda again. After a heart-warming ceremony at the orphanage, there was a phone call for Bob. It was the President of Uganda. The President had heard about the gifts to the orphans and called to thank Bob personally on behalf of his country. The President also invited Bob back to visit him that afternoon. When Bob arrived, the President was in the middle of rushing out of his office. He apologized as he had appointments and invited Bob to come along so they could get acquainted in the car. Along the way, at one of the stops, Bob looked out the window to see what appeared to be a stockyard; only this was not filled with cattle, but with men. Bob asked the President what he was seeing.

The President responded that it was a political prison and those men were his political enemies. The conversation went something like this:

"But Mr. President, it's not right having men living in such horrible conditions. You must let them go."

"But those are my political enemies, men who have tried to subvert my authority. I cannot let them go."

"You have to let them go, it's not right that human beings would have to live in those conditions."

The conversation did not last long, and shortly thereafter, Bob was back in the United States. About a week later, he received a phone call. This time it was from the State Department asking him to come to a meeting with the Under-Secretary for African Affairs. At the meeting, the Under-Secretary and Bob had a conversation along these lines: "Mr. Hunter, on behalf of the Government of the United States, I want to thank you for what you've done in Uganda."

"What? The U.S. Government is thanking me for sending some toys to some orphans in Uganda?"

"No. The President of Uganda recently released his political prisoners, which is something our government has been trying to get him to do for years, without success. He told us that he was doing it because of what you said to him."

Needless to say, Bob Hunter was flabbergasted. But the story doesn't end there. After the State Department meeting, the President of Uganda phoned Bob and asked him to return to Uganda to help him form a new Cabinet for his country.

"But Mr. President, I don't know anything about your country or the people who best serve in your government. I'm just an American businessman. How can I possibly help you choose a Cabinet?"

Bob went and did what he could to help the President select his new ministers. A close friendship has developed between Bob Hunter, American Businessman and the President of Uganda. The President even stays in Bob's home in the D.C. area when he visits the U.S. And you can guess, after those 45 days of praying "God help Africa," Bob Hunter sent Doug Coe a check for $500.

That night Doug told us that he told his story to a group of around 20 very successful business executives, all members of Young Presidents Organization, an international association of business people who have become the chief executives or owners of companies above a certain size by the age of 40. After he told his story at the YPO lunch, 13 of them came up to him and asked if he would take on the bet with them. Swallowing hard, after doing some quick math, he accepted. He laid out the ground rules for them; that they had to pray every day for 45 days. They did not have to tell him what they were praying for, and at the end of the 45 days, it would be entirely up to them to decide whether a mountain had moved as a result of their prayers.

After those 45 days, Doug received 12 checks for $500 each. A while later, he received the 13th check, accompanied by a letter that went something like this: "Doug, my mountain didn't move but the discipline of praying everyday for 45 days has changed my life, so I feel I owe you this $500."

- Contributed Anonymously

"Divine aid is available to those who seek it from their hearts,
humbly and devoutly, through fervent prayer."
- St. Bonaventure

The Power of Prayer—Part 2

Have you ever felt the urge to pray for someone and then just put it on a list and said, "I'll pray for him later."? Or has anyone ever called you and said, "I need you to pray for me, I have this need..."? Read the following story that was sent to me and it may change the way you think about prayer, as well as the way that you pray.

A missionary on furlough told this true story while visiting his home church in Michigan...

"While serving at a small field hospital in Africa, every two weeks I traveled by bicycle through the jungle to a nearby city for supplies. This was a journey of two days and required camping overnight at the halfway point. On one of these journeys, I arrived in the city where I planned to collect money from a bank, purchase medicine and supplies, and then begin my two-day journey back to the field hospital. Upon arrival in the city, I observed two men fighting, one of whom had been seriously injured. I treated him for his injuries and at the same time talked to him about God. I then traveled two days, camping overnight, and arrived home without incident.

Two weeks later, I repeated my journey. Upon arriving in the city, I was approached by the young man I had treated. He told me that he had known I carried money and medicines. He said, 'Some friends and I followed you into the jungle, knowing you would camp overnight. We planned to kill you and take your money and drugs. But just as we were about to move into your camp, we saw that you were surrounded by 26 armed guards.' At this I laughed and said that I was certainly all alone out in that jungle campsite. The young man pressed the point, however, and said, 'No sir, I was not the only person to see the guards. My five friends also saw them, and we all counted them. It was because of those guards that we were afraid and left you alone.'"

At this point in the sermon, one of the men in the congregation jumped to his feet and interrupted the missionary and asked if he could tell him the exact day this happened. The missionary told the congregation the date and the man who interrupted told him this story:

"On the night of your incident in Africa, it was morning here and I was preparing to go play golf. I was about to putt when I felt the urge to pray for you. In fact, the urging was so strong I called men in this church to meet with me here in the sanctuary to pray for you. Would all of those men who met with me on that day stand up?"

The men who had met together that day stood up. The missionary wasn't concerned with who they were—he was too busy counting how many men he saw. There were 26.

This story is an incredible example of how Spirit moves in mysterious ways. If you ever hear such prodding, go along with it. Nothing is ever hurt by prayer, but you cannot imagine the good that could come from it.

- Contributed Anonymously

"A heart-felt prayer is not recitation with the lips. It is a yearning from within which expresses itself in every word, every act, nay every thought of man."
- Mahatma Gandhi

The Lonely Road

A man was driving home one evening on a two-lane country road. Work in this small mid-western community was almost as slow as his beat-up Pontiac, but he never quit looking. Ever since the factory closed, he'd been unemployed, and with winter raging on, the chill had finally hit home.

It was a lonely road. Not very many people had a reason to be on it, unless they were leaving town. Most of his friends had already left. They had families to feed and dreams to fulfill. But he stayed on. After all, this was where he buried his mother and father. He was born here and he knew the country. He could go down this road blind and tell you what was on either side, and with his headlights not working, that came in handy.

It was starting to get dark and light snow flurries were coming down. He figured he'd better get a move on. He almost didn't see the old lady stranded on the side of the road, but when he did, he could see she needed help. He pulled up in front of her Mercedes and got out. His Pontiac was still sputtering when he approached her. Even with the smile on his face, she was worried. No one had stopped to help for the last hour, or so. Was he going to hurt her? He didn't look safe; he looked poor and hungry.

He could see that she was frightened, standing out there in the cold. He knew how she felt. It was that chill which only fear can put in you. "I'm here to help you ma'am. Why don't you wait in the car where it's warm? By the way, my name is Brian." Well, all she had was a flat tire, but for an old lady, that was bad enough.

Brian crawled under the car looking for a place to put the jack, skinning his knuckles a time or two. Soon he was able to change the tire but he was all dirty and his hands hurt. As he was tightening up the lug nuts, she rolled down the window and began to talk to him. She told him she was from St. Louis and was just passing through. She couldn't thank him enough for coming to her aid. Brian just smiled as he closed her trunk. She asked him how much she owed him. Any amount would have been all right with her. She had already imagined all the awful things that could have happened had he not stopped.

Brian never thought twice about the money. This was not a job to him. This was helping someone in need, and God knows there were plenty who had given him a hand in the past. He had lived his whole life that way, and it never occurred to him to act any other way. He told her that if she really wanted to pay him back, the next time she saw someone who needed help, she could give that person the assistance they needed, and Brian added "...and think of me." He waited until she started her car and drove off. It had been a cold and depressing day, but he felt good as he headed for home, disappearing into the twilight.

A few miles down the road, the lady saw a small café. She went in to grab a bite to eat and take the chill off before she made the last leg of her trip home. It was a dingy looking restaurant. Outside were two old gas pumps. The cash register was like the telephone of an out-of-work actor, it didn't ring much. Her waitress came over and brought a clean towel to wipe her wet hair. She had a sweet smile, one that even being on her feet all day couldn't erase. The lady noticed that the waitress was nearly eight months pregnant, but she never let the strain and aches change her attitude. The old lady wondered how someone who had so little could be so giving to a stranger. Then she remembered Brian. After the lady finished her meal and the waitress went to get change for her hundred-dollar bill, the lady slipped right out the door. She was gone by the time the waitress came back. She wondered where the lady could be, then she noticed something written on the napkin under which were four $100 bills. There were tears in her eyes when she read what the lady wrote. It said, "You don't owe me anything. I've been there, too. Somebody once helped me out the way I'm helping you. If you really want to pay me back, here is what you do. Do not let this chain of love end with you."

Well there were tables to clear, sugar bowls to fill, and people to serve, but the waitress made it through another day. That night when she got home from work and climbed into bed, she was thinking about the money and what the lady had written. How could the lady have known how much she and her husband needed it? With the baby due next month, it was going to be hard. She knew how worried her husband was, and as he lay sleeping next to her, she gave him a soft kiss and whispered in his ear, "Everything's gonna be all right; I love you, Brian."

- Contributed Anonymously

"Down in their hearts, wise men know this truth: the only way to help yourself is to help others."
- Elbert Hubbard

The Ant and the Contact Lens

Brenda was a young woman who was invited to go rock climbing. Although she was scared to death, she went with her group to a tremendous granite cliff. In spite of her fear, she put on the gear, took a hold of the rope, and started up the face of that rock. After a short time, she got to a ledge where she could take a breather. As she was hanging on there, the safety rope snapped against Brenda's eye and knocked out her contact lens. Well, here she is on a rock ledge, with hundreds of feet below her and hundreds of feet above her. Of course, she looked and looked and looked, hoping it had landed on the ledge, but it just wasn't there.

Here she was, far from home, her sight now blurry. She was desperate and began to get upset, so she prayed to God to help her find it. When she got to the top, a friend examined her eye and her clothing for the lens, but there was no contact lens to be found. She sat down, despondent, with the rest of the party, waiting for the others to make it up the face of the cliff. She looked out across range after range of mountain, thinking of that Bible verse that says, "The eyes of the Lord run to and fro throughout the whole earth." She thought, "God, You can see all these mountains. You know every stone and leaf, and You know exactly where my contact lens is. Please help me."

Finally, they walked down the trail to the bottom. At the bottom there was a new party of climbers just starting up the face of the cliff. One of them shouted, "Hey you guys! Anybody lose a contact lens?"

Well, that would be startling enough, but you know why the climber saw it? An ant was moving slowly across the face of the rock, carrying it.

Brenda told me that her father is a cartoonist. When she told him the incredible story of the ant, the prayer, and the contact lens, he drew a picture of an ant lugging that contact lens with the words, "God, I don't know why You want me to carry this thing. I can't eat it, and it's awfully heavy. But if this is what You want me to do, I'll carry it for You."

I think it would probably do some of us good to occasionally say, "God, I don't know why You want me to carry this load. I can see no good in it and it's awfully heavy. But, if You want me to carry it, I will." God doesn't call the qualified, He qualifies the called.

- Contributed Anonymously

"If you are given to worry and anxiety, think about the fearless confidence and trust of the Spirit. This will at once relieve your mind of the thoughts that have stirred you, and the power of Spirit will begin its work of straightening out your affairs."
- Charles Fillmore

The Boy with the Giant Heart

It was one of the hottest days of the dry season. We had not seen rain in almost a month. The crops were dying. Cows had stopped giving milk. The creeks and streams were long gone back into the earth. It was a dry season that would bankrupt seven farmers before it was through. Every day, my husband and his brothers would go about the arduous process of trying to get water to the fields. Lately, this process had involved taking a truck to the local water rendering plant and filling it with water. But severe rationing had cut everyone off. If we didn't see some rain soon, we would lose everything. It was on this day that I learned the true lesson of sharing and witnessed the only miracle I have seen with my own eyes.

I was in the kitchen making lunch for my husband and his brothers when I saw my six-year old son, Billy, walking towards the woods. He wasn't walking with the usual carefree abandon of a child, but with a serious purpose. I could only see his back. He was obviously walking with a great effort, trying to be as still as possible. Minutes after he disappeared into the woods, he came running out again, toward the house. I went back to making sandwiches, thinking that whatever task he had been doing was completed. Moments later, however, he was once again walking in that slow purposeful stride toward the woods. This activity went on for an hour: walk carefully to the woods, run back to the house. Finally, I couldn't take it any longer and I crept out of the house and followed him on his journey (being very careful not to be seen...as he was obviously doing important work and didn't need his Mommy checking up on him). He was cupping both hands in front of him as he walked; being very careful not to spill the water he held in them...maybe two or three tablespoons were held in his tiny hands. I sneaked close as he went into the woods. Branches and thorns slapped his little face but he did not try to avoid them. He had a much higher purpose.

As I leaned in to spy on him, I saw the most amazing site. Several large deer loomed in front of him. Billy walked right up to them. I almost screamed for him to get away. A huge buck with elaborate antlers was dangerously close. But the buck did not threaten him...he didn't even move as Billy knelt down. And I saw a tiny fawn lying on the ground, obviously suffering from dehydration and heat exhaustion, lift its head with great effort to lap up the water cupped in my beautiful boy's hands. When the water was gone, Billy jumped up to run back to the house and I hid behind a tree. I followed him back to the house; to a spigot that we had shut off the water to. Billy opened it all the way up and a small trickle began to creep out. He knelt there, letting the drip slowly fill up his makeshift "cup" as the sun beat down on his little back. And it became clear to me—the trouble he had gotten into for playing with the hose the week before and the lecture he had received about the importance of not wasting water were the reasons he didn't ask me to help him.

It took almost twenty minutes for the drops to fill his hands. When he stood up and began the trek back, I was there in front of him. His little eyes just filled with tears. "I'm not wasting," was all he said.

As he began his walk, I joined him...with a small pot of water from the kitchen. I let him tend to the fawn. I stayed away. It was his job. I stood on the edge of the woods watching the most beautiful heart I have ever known working so hard to save another life. As the tears that rolled down my face began to hit the ground they were suddenly joined by other drops...and more drops...and more. I looked up at the sky. It was as if God, Himself, was weeping with pride.

Some will probably say that this was all just a huge coincidence; that miracles don't really exist; that it was bound to rain sometime. And I can't argue with that...I'm not going to try. All I can say is that the rain that came that day saved our farm...just like the actions of one little boy saved a life.

- Contributed Anonymously

"You will find, as you look back upon your life, that the moments that stand out are the moments when you have done things for others."
- Henry Drummond

Lost and Found

John Powell, a Professor at Loyola University, writes about a student in his Theology of Faith class named Tommy:

Some twelve years ago, I stood watching my university students file into the classroom for our first session of class. That was the day I first saw Tommy. My eyes and my mind both blinked. He was combing his long flaxen hair, which hung six inches below his shoulders. It was the first time I had ever seen a boy with hair that long. I guess it was just coming into fashion then. I know in my mind that it isn't what's on your head but what's in it that counts; but on that day I was unprepared and my emotions flipped. I immediately filed Tommy under "S" for strange...very strange. Tommy turned out to be the "atheist in residence" in my Theology of Faith course. He constantly objected to, smirked at, or whined about the possibility of an unconditionally loving Father-God.

We lived with each other in relative peace for one semester, although I admit he was for me, at times, a serious pain in the back pew. When he came up at the end of the course to turn in his final exam, he asked in a slightly cynical tone: "Do you think I'll ever find God?"

I decided instantly on a little shock therapy. "No!" I said very emphatically.

"Oh," he responded, "I thought that was the product you were pushing."

I let him get five steps from the classroom door and then called out: "Tommy! I don't think you'll ever find Him, but I am absolutely certain that He will find you!" He shrugged a little and left my class and my life. I felt slightly disappointed at the thought that he had missed my clever line: "He will find you!" At least I thought it was clever. Later I heard that Tommy had graduated and I was duly grateful.

Then a sad report, three years later I heard that Tommy had terminal cancer. Before I could search him out, he came to see me. When he walked into my office, his body was very badly wasted, and the long hair had all fallen out as a result of chemotherapy. But his eyes were bright and his voice was firm, for the first time, I believe.

"Tommy, I've thought about you so often. I hear you're sick!" I blurted out.

"Oh, yes, very sick. I have cancer in both lungs. It's a matter of weeks."

"Can you talk about it, Tom?"

"Sure, what would you like to know?"

"What's it like to be only twenty-four and dying?

"Well, it could be worse."

"Like what?"

"Well, like being fifty and having no values or ideals, like being fifty and thinking booze, seducing women, and making money are the real 'biggies' in life."

I began to look through my mental file cabinet under "S" where I had filed Tommy as strange. (It seems as though everybody I try to reject by classification God sends back into my life to educate me.)

"But what I really came to see you about," Tom said, "is something you said to me on the last day of class." (He remembered!) He continued, "I asked you if you thought I would ever find God and you said, 'No!' which surprised me. Then you said, 'But He will find you.' I thought about that a lot, even though my search for God was hardly intense at that time. But when the doctors removed a lump from my groin and told me that it was malignant, then I got serious about locating God. And when the malignancy spread into my vital organs, I really began banging bloody fists against the bronze door of Heaven. But God did not come out. In fact, nothing happened. Did you ever try anything for a long time with great effort and with no success? You get psychologically whipped, fed up with trying. And then you quit. Well, one day I woke up, and instead of throwing a few more futile appeals over that high brick wall to a God who may or may not be there, I just quit. I decided that I didn't really care...about God, about an afterlife, or anything like that. I decided to spend the time I had left doing something more profitable. I thought about your class and I remembered something else you said: 'The essential sadness is to go through life without loving. But it would be almost equally sad to go through life and leave this world without ever telling those you loved that you had loved them.'

So I began with the hardest one: my Dad. He was reading the newspaper when I approached him. 'Dad...'

'Yes, what?' he asked without lowering the newspaper.

'Dad, I'd like to talk with you.'

'Well, talk.'

'I mean...it's really important.' The newspaper came down three slow inches.

'What is it?'

'Dad, I love you. I just wanted you to know that.'" Tom smiled at me and said with obvious satisfaction, as though he felt a warm and secret joy flowing inside of him.

"The newspaper fluttered to the floor. Then my father did two things I could never remember him ever doing before. He cried and he hugged me. And we talked all night, even though he had to go to work the next morning. It felt so good to be close to my father, to see his tears, to feel his hug, to hear him say that he loved me.

It was easier with my mother and little brother. They cried with me, too, and we hugged each other, and started saying real nice things to each other. We shared the things we had been keeping secret for so many years. I was only sorry about one thing: that I had waited so long. Here I was just beginning to open up to all the people I had actually been close to.

Then, one day I turned around and God was there. He didn't come to me when I pleaded with Him. I guess I was like an animal trainer holding out a hoop, 'C'mon, jump through. I'll give you three days.' Apparently God does things in His own way and at His own hour. But the important thing is that He was there. He found me. You were right. He found me even after I stopped looking for Him."

"Tommy," I practically gasped, "I think you are saying something very important and much more universal than you realize. To me, at least, you're saying the surest way to find God is not to make Him a private possession, a problem solver, or an instant consolation in times of need, but rather by opening to love. You know, the Apostle John said that God is love, and anyone who lives in love is living with God and God is living in him. Tom, could I ask you a favor? You know, when I had you in class you were a real pain. But (laughingly) you can make it all up to me now. Would you come into my present Theology of Faith course and tell them what you've just told me? If I told them the same thing, it wouldn't be nearly as effective as if you were to tell them."

"Oooh...I was ready for you, but I don't know if I'm ready for your class."

"Tom, think about it. If and when you're ready, give me a call."

In a few days, Tommy called, and said he was ready for the class, that he wanted to do that for God and for me. So we scheduled a date. However, he never made it. He had another appointment, far more important than the one with me and my class. Of course, his life was not really ended by his death, only changed. He made the great step from faith into vision. He found a life far more beautiful than the eye of man has ever seen or the ear of man has ever heard or the mind of man has ever imagined.

Before he died, we talked one last time. "I'm not going to make it to your class," he said.

"I know, Tom."

"Will you tell them for me? Will you...tell the whole world for me?"

"I will, Tom. I'll tell them. I'll do my best."

- Contributed Anonymously

"We should live in such a way that in our last hours we will not regret having loved too little."
- Chiara Lubich

The Last Ride

Twenty years ago, I drove a cab for a living. It was a cowboy's life, a life for someone who wanted no boss. What I didn't realize was that it was also a ministry. Because I drove the night shift, my cab became a moving confessional. Passengers climbed in, sat behind me in total anonymity, and told me about their lives. I encountered people whose lives amazed me, enabled me, made me laugh and weep. But none touched me more than a woman I picked up late one August night.

I was responding to a call from a small brick four-plex in a quiet part of town. I assumed I was being sent to pick up some party people, or someone who had just had a fight with a lover, or a worker heading to an early shift at some factory in the industrial part of town.

When I arrived at 2:30 a.m., the building was dark except for a single light in a ground floor window. Under such circumstances, many drivers just honk once or twice, wait a minute, then drive away. But I had seen too many impoverished people who depended on taxis as their only means of transportation. Unless a situation smelled of danger, I always went to the door. This passenger might be someone who needs my assistance, I reasoned to myself. So I walked to the door and knocked.

"Just a minute," answered a frail, elderly voice. I could hear something being dragged across the floor. After a long pause, the door opened. A small woman in her 80's stood before me. She was wearing a print dress and a pillbox hat with a veil pinned on it, like somebody out of a 1940's movie. By her side was a small nylon suitcase. The apartment looked as if no one had lived in it for years. All the furniture was covered with sheets. There were no clocks on the walls, no knickknacks or utensils on the counters. In the corner was a cardboard box filled with photos and glassware.

"Would you carry my bag out to the car?" she asked.

I took the suitcase to the cab, then returned to assist the woman. She took my arm and we walked slowly toward the curb. She kept thanking me for my kindness. "It's nothing," I told her. "I just try to treat my passengers the way I would want my mother treated."

"Oh, you're such a good boy," she said. When we got in the cab, she gave me an address, then asked, "Can you drive through downtown?"

"It's not the shortest way," I answered quickly.

"Oh, I don't mind," she said. "I'm in no hurry. I'm on my way to a hospice." I looked in the rearview mirror. Her eyes were glistening. "I don't have any family left," she continued. "The doctor says I don't have very long."

I quietly reached over and shut off the meter. "What route would you like me to take?" I asked.

For the next two hours, we drove thought the city. She showed me the building where she had once worked as an elevator operator. We drove through the neighborhood where she and her husband had lived when they were newlyweds. She had me pull up in front of a furniture warehouse that had once been a ballroom where she had gone dancing as a girl. Sometimes she'd ask me to slow down in front of a particular building or corner and would sit staring into the darkness, saying nothing. As the first hint of sun was creasing into the horizon, she suddenly said, "I'm tired. Let's go now."

We drove in silence to the address she had given me. It was a low building, like a small convalescent home, with a driveway that passed under a portico. Two orderlies came out to the cab as soon as we pulled up. They were solicitous and intent, watching her every move. They must have been expecting her. I opened the trunk and took the small suitcase to the door. The woman was already seated in a wheelchair.

"How much do I owe you?" she asked, reaching into her purse.

"Nothing," I said.

"You have to make a living," she answered.

"There are other passengers," I responded. Almost without thinking, I bent over and gave her a big hug. She held onto me tightly.

"You gave an old woman a little moment of joy," she said. "Thank you."

I squeezed her hand, then walked into the dim morning light. Behind me, a door shut. It was the sound of the closing of a life. I didn't pick up any more passengers that shift. I drove aimlessly, lost in thought. For the rest of that day, I could hardly talk. What if that woman had gotten an angry driver, or one who was impatient to end his shift? What if I had refused to take the run, or had honked once, then driven away?

On a quick review, I don't think that I have done anything more important in my life. We're conditioned to think that our lives revolve around great moments. But great moments catch us unaware...beautifully wrapped in what others may consider a small one.

- Contributed Anonymously

"No act of kindness, no matter how small, is ever wasted."
- Aesop

Angels in the Classroom

A pastor read a letter from an elementary school teacher who attends East Hill church. The gist of the letter was as follows:

Last school year, her classroom was made up of little third graders, every one of which came from either a single parent family, or a dysfunctional family, was undernourished and/or uncared for, lived in an abusive home and was either beaten, bruised, or raped by other family members; one little girl's dad died of AIDS, and the list goes on. Her heart bled for these kids. Before the '99—'00 school year started, she and her husband went to her classroom and prayed over each desk in the room. They prayed that God would place an angel behind each and every child throughout the coming year to watch over them and protect them.

A month or so after the year had started, she gave the kids an assignment to write about what they would like to be when they grew up. Everybody was busy with his or her assignment when Andrew raised his hand. When she asked him what he needed, he asked how to spell "mighty." After telling him how to spell "mighty," she asked him why he needed to know. Andrew said it was because when he grew up he wanted to be a "mighty man of God."

When he said this, little Mark sitting next to him asked, "So, what's a mighty man of God?" The teacher, swallowing back her tears, and knowing she could not say anything in the classroom, told Andrew to go ahead and tell Mark what it was.

So Andrew says, "It's a man who puts on the armor of God and is a soldier for God."

After observing some conversation between Andrew and Mark, the teacher, with a lump in her throat, started to walk away when Andrew motioned his little forefinger for her to come closer. He whispered to her, asking if she believed in angels. She told him yes, she did. Then he asked her if she thought people could see angels, and she said she thought some people probably could. Andrew said that he did, and he could see an angel standing behind each kid in the room.

- Contributed Anonymously

"For every soul, there is a Guardian watching it."
- The Koran

The Tablecloth

The brand new pastor and his wife, newly assigned to their first ministry to reopen a church in urban Brooklyn, arrived in early October excited about their opportunities. When they saw their church, it was very run down and needed much work. They set a goal to have everything done in time to have their first service on Christmas Eve.

They worked hard, repairing pews, plastering walls, painting, etc., and on December 18th found themselves ahead of schedule and just about finished. On December 19th, a terrible driving rainstorm hit the area and lasted for two days. On the 21st, the pastor went over to the church. His heart sank when he saw that the roof had leaked, causing a large area of plaster about 6 feet by 8 feet to fall off the front wall of the sanctuary just behind the pulpit, beginning about head high. The pastor cleaned up the mess on the floor, and not knowing what else to do but postpone the Christmas Eve service, headed home. On the way, he noticed that a local business was having a flea market type sale for charity so he stopped in. One of the items was a beautiful, handmade, ivory colored, crocheted tablecloth with exquisite work, fine colors and a cross embroidered right in the center. It was just the right size to cover up the hole in the front wall. He bought it and headed back to the church.

By this time it had started to snow. An older woman running from the opposite direction was trying to catch the bus. She missed it. The pastor invited her to wait in the warm church for the next bus 45 minutes later. She sat in a pew and paid no attention to the pastor while he got a ladder, hangers and the necessary tools to put up the tablecloth as a wall tapestry. The pastor could hardly believe how beautiful it looked and it covered up the entire problem area. Then he noticed the woman walking down the center aisle. Her face was like a sheet.

"Pastor," she asked, "where did you get that tablecloth?"

The pastor explained. The woman asked him to check the lower right corner to see if the initials, EBG were sewn into it there. They were. These were her initials and she had made this tablecloth 35 years before in Austria. The woman could hardly believe it as the pastor told her how he had just gotten the tablecloth.

The woman explained that before the war, she and her husband were well-to-do people in Austria. When the Nazis came, she was forced to leave. Her husband was going to follow her the next week. She was captured, sent to prison and never saw her husband or her home again.

The pastor wanted to give her the tablecloth; but she made the pastor keep it for the church. The pastor insisted on driving her home; that was the least he could do. She lived on the other side of Staten Island and was only in Brooklyn for the day for a housecleaning job.

What a wonderful service they had on Christmas Eve. The church was almost full. The music and the spirit were great. At the end of the service, the pastor and his wife greeted everyone at the door and many said they would return.

One older man, whom the pastor recognized from the

neighborhood, continued to sit on the pews and stare, and the pastor wondered why he wasn't leaving. The man asked him where he got the tablecloth on the front wall because it was identical to one that his wife had made years ago when they lived in Austria before the war and how could there be two tablecloths so much alike? He told the pastor how the Nazis came, how he forced his wife to flee for her safety, and he was supposed to follow her, but he was arrested and put in a concentration camp. He never saw his wife or his home again.

The pastor asked him if he would allow him to take him for a little ride. They drove to Staten Island to the same house where the pastor had taken the woman three days earlier. He helped the man climb the three flights of stairs to the woman's apartment, knocked on the door and he saw the greatest Christmas reunion he could ever imagine.

- Contributed Anonymously

"Be patient; everything will unfold in due season."
- Joseph Girzone

— Part 4—

Modern Day Parables

Throughout history, the deepest Truths were taught through parables. These modern day stories do the same, as they find a beautiful way to teach us all what we need to learn to enhance our lives, as well as the lives of others.

Desire the "Secrets"

There once was this great teacher who had many disciples dedicated to learning truth. One day one of his students came to him and said, "Master, all I want is to be as peaceful as you. Please give me the secret to your enlightenment."

The teacher stood up and walked away without saying a word.

A week later that same student came to him and said, "Master, all I want is to be enlightened like you. Do not withhold your secret from me."

Again the teacher turned his back on the student.

After another week the student again said, "Master, I know that you have the secret that I seek. I will not rest until you give it to me."

This time the teacher asked the student to follow him down the path to the river. The teacher took off his clothes and jumped in. He told the student to do the same. The young man jumped into the river but before he was able to get his feet beneath him, the teacher grabbed him and held him under the water. The student struggled and fought, but the teacher was too strong for him. Finally the teacher let go and the student came up gasping for air. After a moment the teacher said, "When you were beneath the water, what was the one thing on your mind?"

The student wiped the water from his eyes and said, "Getting a breath of air. All I could think about was air."

The teacher then looked deep into his eyes. "When you want enlightenment the same way you wanted air, I won't have to tell you anything. Then you will tell me."

"Every man must find his own philosophy....
.his attitude toward life."
-Lin Yutang

First Struggle, Then Fly

A man found a cocoon of a butterfly. One day a small opening appeared. He sat and watched the butterfly for several hours as it struggled to force its body through that little hole. Then it seemed as if it had stopped making any progress. It appeared as if it had gotten as far as it could, and it could go no further. The man decided to help the butterfly, so he took a pair of scissors and gently snipped off the remaining bit of the cocoon. The butterfly emerged easily, but it had a swollen body and small, shriveled wings. The man continued to watch the butterfly because he expected that, at any moment, the wings would enlarge and expand in order to support the body, which would contract in time. Neither happened. In fact, the butterfly spent the rest of its life crawling around with a swollen body and shriveled wings. It was never able to fly.

What the man, in his kindness and haste, did not understand was that the restricting cocoon and the struggle required for the butterfly to get through the tiny opening were God's way of forcing fluid from the body of the butterfly into its wings so that it would be ready for flight once it achieved its freedom from the cocoon.

Sometimes, struggles are exactly what we need in our life. If God allowed us to go through our life without any obstacles, it would cripple us. We would not be as strong as we could have been, and we could never fly. So don't be so anxious to get rid of the struggles in your life. Embrace them, learn from them, and fly.

"God allows us to experience the low points of life in order to teach us lessons we could not learn in any other way."
- C. S. Lewis

How Do You Live Your Dash?

I read of a man who stood to speak
At the funeral of a friend.
He referred to the dates on her tombstone
From the beginning....to the end.
He noted that first came her date of birth
And spoke the following date with tears,
But he said what mattered most of all
Was the dash between those years (1930—1997).
For that dash represents all the time
That she spent alive on earth.
And now only those who loved her
Know what that little line is worth.
For it matters not how much we own,
The cars...the house...the cash,
What matters is how we live and love
And how we spend our dash.
So think about this long and hard,
Are there things you'd like to change?
For you never know how much time is left,
That can still be rearranged.
If we could just slow down enough
To consider what's true and real
And always understand
The way other people feel.
And be less quick to anger,
And show appreciation more
And love the people in our lives
Like we've never loved before.

If we treat each other with respect,
And more often wear a smile...
Remembering that this special dash
Might only last a little while.
So, when your eulogy's being read
With your life's actions to rehash,
Would you be proud of the things they say
About how you spent your dash?

"I don't know what tomorrow will bring - except old age and death - but I do know that I do have today, one absolutely glorious day that I will savor and make the most of as if it were my last one....because it may be."
- Gary W. Fenchuk

Things Aren't Always What They Seem

Some traveling angels stopped to spend the night in the home of a wealthy family. The family was rude and refused to let the angels stay in the mansion's guest room. Instead, the angels were given a space in the cold basement. As they made their bed on the hard floor, the older angel saw a hole in the wall and repaired it. When the younger angel asked why, the older angel replied......"Things aren't always what they seem."

The next night, the pair came to rest at the house of a very poor, but hospitable farmer and his wife. After sharing what little food they had, the couple let the angels sleep in their bed where they could have a good night's rest.

When the sun came up the next morning, the angels found

the farmer and his wife in tears. Their only cow, whose milk was their sole income, lay dead in the field. The younger angel was infuriated and asked the older angel, "How could you have let this happen? The first man had everything, yet you helped him," she accused. "The second family had little but was willing to share everything, and you let their cow die."

"Things aren't always what they seem," the older angel replied. "When we stayed in the basement of the mansion, I noticed there was gold stored in that hole in the wall. Since the owner was so obsessed with greed and unwilling to share his good fortune, I sealed the wall so he wouldn't find it. Then last night, as we slept in the farmer's bed, the angel of death came for his wife. I gave her the cow instead. You see, things aren't always what they seem."

Sometimes, this is exactly what happens when things don't turn out the way they should. If you have faith in God, just trust that every outcome is always to your advantage. You might not realize it until later.

"Looking back, we see with great clarity, and what once appeared as difficulties now reveal themselves as blessings."
– Dan Millman

―――――――――――

Blessings in Disguise

A parable is told of a farmer who owned an old mule. The mule fell into the farmer's well. After carefully assessing the situation, the farmer sympathized with the mule, but decided that neither the mule nor the well was worth the trouble of saving. He called his neighbors together and enlisted them to help haul dirt to bury the old mule in the well and put him out of his misery.

Initially, the old mule was hysterical. But as the farmer and his neighbors continued shoveling, the dirt hit the mule's back. It suddenly dawned on him that every time a shovel load of dirt landed on his back, he should shake it off and step up. This he did, blow after blow. "Shake it off and step up....shake it off and step up....shake it off and step up." He repeated it to encourage himself. No matter how painful the blows, or distressing the situation seemed, the old mule fought "panic." He just kept right on shaking it off and stepping up!

It wasn't long before the old mule, battered and exhausted, stepped triumphantly over the wall of that well. What seemed like it would bury him, actually blessed him....all because of the manner in which he handled his adversity.

If we face our problems and respond to them positively, and refuse to give in to panic, bitterness, or self-pity....the adversities that come along to bury us usually have within them the potential to benefit and bless us.

"Many men owe the grandeur of their lives to their tremendous difficulties."
- Charles H. Spurgeon

God Are You Real?

The little child whispered,
"God, speak to me."
And a meadowlark sang.
But the child did not hear.

So the child yelled,
"God, speak to me!"
And the thunder rolled across the sky,
But the child did not listen.

The child looked around and said
"God, let me see you."
And a star shone brightly
But the child did not notice.

And the child shouted,
"God, show me a miracle!"
And a life was born
But the child did not know.

So the child cried out in despair,
"Touch me God, and let me know you are here!"
Whereupon God reached down
And touched the child.
But the child brushed the butterfly away
And walked away unknowingly.

Take time to listen. Often times, the things we seek are right beneath our noses. Don't miss out on your blessing because it isn't packaged the way that you expect.

"The great blessings of mankind are within us, and within our reach; but we shut our eyes and, like people in the dark, fall short of the very thing we search for without finding it."
- Seneca

Put Your BIG ROCKS in First

One day an expert in time management was speaking to a group of business students and, to drive home a point, used an illustration those students will never forget. As he stood in front of the group of high-powered overachievers he said, "Okay, time for a quiz." Then he pulled out a one-gallon, wide-mouth mason jar and set it on the table. Then he produced about a dozen fist-sized rocks and carefully placed them into the jar. When the jar was filled to the top, he asked, "Is the jar full?"

Everyone in the class said, "Yes."

He said, "Really?" He reached under the table and pulled out a bucket of gravel. Then he dumped some gravel in and shook the jar causing pieces of gravel to work themselves down into the space between the big rocks. Then he asked the group once more, "Is the jar full?"

By this time the class was on to him. "Probably not," one of them answered.

"Good," he replied. He reached under the table and brought out a bucket of sand. He started dumping the sand in the jar and it went into all of the spaces left between the rocks and gravel. Once more he asked the question, "Is the jar full?"

"No!" the class shouted.

Once again he said, "Good." Then he grabbed a pitcher of water and began to pour it in until the jar was filled to the brim. Then he looked at the class and asked, "What is the point of this illustration?"

One student raised his hand and said, "The point is, no matter how full your schedule is, if you try really hard you can always fit some more things in it!"

"No," the speaker replied, "that's not the point. The truth this illustration teaches us is: If you don't put the big rocks in first, you'll never get them in at all."

What are the big rocks in your life? Time with your loved ones....Your faith, your education, your dreams....A worthy cause....Teaching or mentoring others. Remember to put these BIG ROCKS in first or you'll never get them all in.

"Live as you will have wished to have lived when you are dying."
                                            - Charles F. Gellert

Two Dogs

A Native American elder was describing his inner struggles:
    "Inside of me there are two dogs. One of the dogs is mean and evil. The other dog is good. The mean dog fights the good dog all the time." When asked which dog wins, he reflected for a moment and replied: "The one I feed the most."

The Voice

There is a voice inside of you
That whispers all day long.
"I feel that this is right for me.
I know that this is wrong."
No teacher, preacher, parent, friend
Or wise man can decide
What's right for you—just listen to
That voice that speaks inside.

"What is Truth? A difficult question; but I have solved it for myself by saying that it is what the "voice within" tells you."
    – Mahatma Gandhi

E-mail from God

As you got up this morning, I watched you and hoped you would talk to me, even if it was just a few words, asking my opinion or thanking me for something good that happened in your life yesterday—but I noticed you were too busy trying to find the right outfit to put on and wear to work. I waited again. When you ran around the house getting ready, I knew there would be a few minutes for you to stop and say hello, but you were too busy. At one point, you had to wait fifteen minutes with nothing to do except sit in a chair. Then I saw you spring to your feet. I thought you wanted to talk to me but you ran to the phone and called a friend to get the latest gossip. I watched as you went to work and I waited patiently all day long. With all your activities, I guess you were too busy to say anything to me. I noticed that before lunch you looked around, maybe you felt embarrassed to talk to me; that's why you didn't bow your head. You glanced at three or four tables and you noticed some of your friends talking to me briefly before they ate, but you didn't. That's okay. There is still more time left, and I have hope that you will talk to me yet.

You went home and it seems as if you had a lot of things to do. After a few of them were done, you turned on the TV. I don't know if you like TV or not, just about anything goes. You spend a lot of time each day in front of it, not thinking about anything—just enjoying the show. I waited patiently again as you watched the TV and ate your meal but again you didn't talk to me. Bedtime I guess you felt too tired. After you said goodnight to your family, you plopped into bed and fell asleep in no time. That's okay because you may not realize that I am always there for you. I have patience more than you will ever know. I even want to teach you how to be patient with others, as well. I love you so much that I wait everyday for a nod, prayer, thought or even a thankful part of your heart. It is hard to have a one-sided conversation.

Well, you are getting up again and, once again, I will wait with nothing but love for you hoping that today you will give me some time. Have a nice day!

Your friend,
GOD

"I always begin my prayer in silence, for it is in the silence of the heart that God speaks. God is the friend of silence—we need to listen to God because it's not what we say, but what He says to us and through us that matters"
— Mother Teresa

The Power of Prayer—Part 3

A voyaging ship was wrecked during a storm at sea and only two of the men on it were able to swim to a small, desert-like island. The two survivors, not knowing what else to do, agreed that they had no other recourse but to pray to God. However, to find out whose prayer was more powerful, they agreed to divide the territory between them and stay on opposite sides of the island.

The first man was hungry so he prayed for food and the next morning, he saw a fruit-bearing tree on his side of the land, and he was able to eat its fruit. The other man's parcel of land remained barren.

After some days, the first man was lonely and he decided to pray for a wife. The next day, another ship was wrecked, and the only survivor was a woman who swam to his side of the island. On the other side of the island, the second man had nothing. Soon the first man prayed for a house, clothes, and more food. The next day, like magic, all of these were given to him. However, the second man still had nothing.

Finally, the first man prayed for a ship, so that he and his wife could leave the island. In the morning, he found a ship docked at his side on the island. The first man boarded the ship with his wife and decided to leave the second man on the island. He considered the other man unworthy to receive God's blessings, since none of his prayers had been answered.

As the ship was about to leave, the first man heard a voice from heaven booming: "Why are you leaving your companion on the island?"

"My blessings are mine alone, since I was the one who prayed for them," the first man replied. "His prayers were all unanswered and so he does not deserve anything."

"You are mistaken," the voice rebuked him. "He had only one prayer, which I answered."

"Tell me," the first man asked the voice, "what did he pray for that I should owe him anything?"

"He prayed that all your prayers be answered."

"Make every effort to pray from the heart. Even if you do not succeed, in the eyes of the Lord the effort is precious."
- The Gates of Prayer

The Mexican Fisherman

An American businessman was at the pier of a small coastal Mexican village when a small boat with just one fisherman docked. Inside the small boat were several large yellow fin tuna. The American complimented the Mexican on the quality of his fish and asked how long it took to catch them. The Mexican replied, "Only a little while."

The American then asked why he didn't stay out longer and catch more fish. The Mexican said he had enough to support his family's immediate needs. The American then asked, "But what do you do with the rest of your time?"

The Mexican fisherman said, "I sleep late, fish a little, play with my children, take siesta with my wife, Maria, stroll into the village each evening where I sip wine and play guitar with my amigos. I have a full and busy life, señor."

The American scoffed, "I am a Harvard MBA and could help you. You should spend more time fishing and with the proceeds buy a bigger boat; with the proceeds from the bigger boat, you could buy several boats; eventually you would have a fleet of fishing boats. Instead of selling your catch to a middleman, you would sell directly to the processor, eventually opening your own cannery. You would control the product, processing and distribution. You would need to leave this small coastal fishing village and move to Mexico City, then LA and eventually NYC, where you will run your expanding enterprise."

The Mexican fisherman asked, "But señor, how long will all this take?" To which the American replied, "15—20 years."

"But what then, señor?"

The American laughed and said, "That's the best part. When the time is right, you would announce an IPO and sell your company stock to the public and become very rich, you would make millions."

"Millions, señor? Then what?"

The American said, "Then you would retire, move to a small coastal village where you would sleep late, fish a little, play with your kids, take siesta with your wife, stroll to the village in the evenings where you could sip wine and play your guitar with your amigos."

"Maybe you are here on earth to learn that life is what you make it, and it's to be enjoyed."
- Dick Sutphen

The Echo of Life

A son and his father were walking in the mountains. Suddenly, his son falls, hurts himself and screams, "AAAAHHHH!!!"

To his surprise, he hears the voice repeating, somewhere in the mountain, "AAAAHHHH!!!"

Curious, he yells, "Who are you?"

He receives the answer, "Who are you?"

Angered at the response, he screams, "Coward!"

He receives the answer, "Coward!"

He looks to his father and asks, "What's going on?"

The father smiles and says, "My son, pay attention." And then he screams to the mountain, "I admire you!"

The voice answers, "I admire you!"

Again the man screams, "You are a champion!"

The voice answers, "You are a champion!"

The boy is surprised but does not understand.

Then the father explains, "People call this ECHO, but really this is LIFE. It gives you back everything you say or do. Our life is simply a reflection of our actions. If you want more love in the world, create more love in your heart. If you want more peace in the world, create more peace in your heart. This relationship applies to everything, in all aspects of life. Life will give you back everything you have given it."

YOUR LIFE IS NOT A COINCIDENCE. IT'S A REFLECTION OF YOU!

"The happiness of your life depends on the quality of your thoughts."
- Marcus Antonius

Good Luck, Bad Luck... Who's To Say?

In an out-of-the-way part of the countryside lived a farmer who one day discovered his cow had gotten out of her pasture and disappeared. As he began searching for her he met his neighbor, who asked where the farmer was going. When he replied that his cow was lost, the neighbor shook his head and said, "That's bad luck."

"Good luck, bad luck. Who's to say?" replied the farmer, who went on his way. Out in the hills beyond the cultivated farmland, he found his cow grazing alongside a beautiful horse, and when he led his cow home the horse followed along behind her.

The next morning his neighbor came by to ask about the cow. Seeing her back in her pasture beside a beautiful horse, he asked the farmer what had happened. The farmer explained that the horse had followed his cow home and the neighbor explained. "That's good luck!"

"Good luck, bad luck. Who's to say?" replied the farmer, and he went on with his chores.

The following day the farmer's son returned home on leave from the army. He immediately tried to ride the beautiful horse but was thrown to the ground and broke his leg. When the neighbor passed by on his way to market and saw the young man sitting on the porch with his leg splinted and bandaged while his father hoed the garden, the neighbor asked what had happened. When he heard, he shook his head. "That's bad luck," he said.

"Good luck, bad luck. Who's to say?" replied the farmer, continuing to hoe his garden.

The next day the boy's unit came marching down the road. Overnight, war had broken out and they were off to battle. When the son couldn't join them, the neighbor, leaning over the fence and calling to the farmer in his field, commented that at least the father was spared losing his son in war. "That's good luck," shouted the neighbor.

"Good luck, bad luck. Who's to say?" replied the farmer who went on plowing and living the simple life he had become known for.

Let's not be too quick to judge whether something is "good" or "bad." Give it time to play itself out and you will see that there is Divine Intelligence behind everything.

"Behind every adversity lies a hidden possibility."
- Sufi saying

The Invitation

A woman came out of her house and saw three old men with long white beards sitting in her front yard. She did not recognize them. She said, "I don't think I know you, but you must be hungry. Please come in and have something to eat."

"Is the man of the house home?" they asked.

"No," she said. "He's out."

"Then we cannot come in," they replied.

In the evening when her husband came home, she told him what had happened. Go tell them I am home and invite them in. The woman went out and invited the men in.

"We don't go into a house together," they replied.

"Why is that?" she wanted to know.

One of the old men explained. "His name is Wealth," he said pointing to one of his friends and said pointing to another one, "He is Success and I am Love." Then he added, "Now go in and discuss with your husband which one of us you want in your home."

The woman went in and told her husband what was said. Her husband was overjoyed. "How nice!!" he said. "Since that is the case, let us invite Wealth. Let him come in and fill our home with wealth."

His wife disagreed. "My dear, why don't we invite Success?"

Their daughter was listening from the other corner of the house. She jumped in with her own suggestion. "Would it not be better to invite Love? Our home will be filled with love."

"Let us heed our daughter's advice," said the husband to his wife. "Go out and invite Love to be our guest."

The woman went out and asked the three old men, "Which of you is Love? Please come in and be our guest."

Love got up and started walking toward the house. The other two also got up and followed him. Surprised, the lady asked Wealth and Success, "I only invited Love, why are you coming in?"

The old men replied together, "If you had invited Wealth or Success, the other two of us would've stayed out, but since you invited Love, wherever he goes, we go with him."

Wherever there is Love there is also wealth and success!!!

"Love is the energizing elixir of the universe, the cause and effect of all harmonies."
- Rumi

Is Your Hut Burning?

The only survivor of a shipwreck was washed up on a small, uninhabited island. He prayed feverishly to God to rescue him, and every day he scanned the horizon for help but none seemed forthcoming. Exhausted, he eventually managed to build a little hut out of driftwood to protect him from the elements and to store his few possessions.

One day, after scavenging for food, he arrived home to find his little hut in flames, the smoke rolling up to the sky. The worst had happened; everything was lost. He was stunned with grief and anger.

"God, how could you do this to me!" he cried.

Early the next day, however, he was awakened by the sound of a ship that was approaching the island. It had come to rescue him.

"How did you know I was here?" asked the weary man of his rescuers.

"We saw your smoke signal," they replied.

It's easy to get discouraged when things are going bad. But we shouldn't lose heart because God is at work in our lives, even in the midst of pain and suffering. Remember, the next time your little hut is burning to the ground, it just may be a smoke signal that summons the grace of God. For all the negative things we have to say to ourselves, God has a positive answer for it.

"A man does not always choose what his guardian angel intends."
- St Thomas Aquinas

Creation: A Sioux Story

The Creator gathered all of Creation and said, "I want to hide something from the humans until they are ready for it. It is the realization that they create their own reality."

The eagle said, "Give it to me, I will take it to the moon."

The Creator said, "No. One day they will go there and find it."

The salmon said, "I will bury it on the bottom of the ocean."

"No. They will go there too."

The buffalo said, "I will bury it on the Great Plains."

The Creator said, "They will cut into the skin of the Earth and find it even there."

Grandmother Mole, who lives in the breast of Mother Earth, and who has no physical eyes but sees with spiritual eyes, said, "Put it inside them."

And the Creator said, "It is done."

"Why does a man go out to look for God? It is your own heart beating and you do not know, you were mistaking it for something outside."
- Vivekananda

Their Young Son

A young couple had a son about 4 years old when his younger sister was born. Being concerned about the boy's feelings towards the new baby made the parents a little on edge, they did not know how he would react.

When the little newborn came home the son was very adamant and asked his parents if he could be alone with his sister. He asked over and over again for a period of weeks. The parents were afraid that he might cause the baby harm if left alone but they finally gave in.

Since the boy was so adamant and the parents were so concerned about the baby, they decided to stand at the door to listen and watch without the boy's knowledge. He put his face really close to his sister's, looked into her eyes and his parents heard him as he asked: "Can you tell me what God looks like? I'm beginning to forget."

"He who aspires the grace of God must be pure, with a heart as innocent as a child's. Purity of heart is to God like a perfume sweet and agreeable."
- St. Nicholas of Flue

Choose Your Words Well

A certain good woman one day said something that hurt her best friend of many years. She regretted it immediately, and would have done anything to have taken the words back. But they were said impulsively, in a moment of thoughtlessness, and as close as she and her friend were, she didn't consider the effects of her words beforehand. What she said hurt the friend so much that this good woman was herself hurt for the pain she caused.

In her effort to undo what she had done, she went to an older, wiser woman in the village. Explaining her situation, she asked for advice. The older woman listened patiently in an effort to determine just how sincere the younger woman was; how far she was willing to go to correct the situation. She explained that sometimes, in order to put things back the way they once were; great efforts must be made. She then asked, "Just what would you be willing to do to repair the harm done?"

The answer was heartfelt. "Anything!"

Listening to her, the older woman sensed the younger woman's distress and knew she must help her. She also knew she could never alleviate her own pain by living her life for her, but she could teach, if the younger woman would first listen, and then learn. She knew the outcome would depend solely on the character of the younger woman. She said, "There are two things needed to do to make amends. The first of the two is extremely difficult. Tonight, take your best feather pillows and open a small hole in each one. Then, before the sun rises, you must put a single feather on the doorstep of each house in town. When you are through, come back to me. If you've done the first thing completely, I'll tell you the second."

The young woman hurried home to prepare for her chore, even though the pillows were very expensive and very dear to her. All night long she labored alone in the cold. She went from doorstep to doorstep, taking care not to overlook a single house. Her fingers were frozen; the wind was so sharp it caused her eyes to water. But she ran on through the darkened streets, thankful there was something she could do to put things back the way they once were. Finally, as the sky was getting light, she placed the last feather on the steps of the last house. Just as the sun rose, she returned to the older woman. She was exhausted, but relieved that her efforts would be rewarded.

"My pillows are empty. I placed a feather on the doorstep of each home."

"Now," said the wise woman, "go back and refill your pillows. Then everything will be as it was before."

The young woman was stunned. "You know that's impossible! The wind blew away each feather as fast as I placed them on the doorsteps!! You didn't say I had to get them back!! If this is the second requirement, then things will never be the same."

"That's true," said the older woman. "Never forget. Each of your words is like a feather in the wind. Once spoken, no amount of effort, regardless of how heartfelt or sincere, can ever return them to your mouth. Choose your words well and guard them most of all in the presence of those you love."

The words of the tongue should have three gatekeepers:
- *Is it true?*
- *Is it kind?*
- *Is it necessary?*
                    - Arabian proverb

The Obstacle in Our Path

In ancient times, a king had a boulder placed on a roadway. Then he hid himself and watched to see if anyone would remove the huge rock. Some of the king's wealthiest merchants and courtiers came by and simply walked around it. Many loudly blamed the king for not keeping the roads clear, but none did anything about getting the big stone out of the way.

Then a peasant came along carrying a load of vegetables. On approaching the boulder, the peasant laid down his burden and tried to move the stone to the side of the road. After much pushing and straining, he finally succeeded. As the peasant picked up his load of vegetables, he noticed a purse lying in the road where the boulder had been. The purse contained many gold coins and a note from the king indicating that the gold was for the person who removed the boulder from the roadway.

The peasant learned what many others never understand. Every obstacle presents an opportunity to improve one's condition.

"We find no real satisfaction or happiness in life without
obstacles to conquer and goals to achieve."
– Dr. Maxwell Maltz

The Three Trees

Once there were three trees on a hill in the woods. They were discussing their hopes and dreams when the first tree said, "Someday I hope to be a treasure chest. I could be filled with gold, silver and precious gems. I could be decorated with intricate carvings and everyone would see the beauty."

Then the second tree said, "Someday I will be a mighty ship. I will take kings and queens across the waters and sail to the corners of the world. Everyone will feel safe in me because of the strength of my hull."

Finally the third tree said, "I want to grow to be the tallest and straightest tree in the forest. People will see me on top of the hill and look up at my branches and think of the heavens and God and how close to them I'm reaching. I will be the greatest tree of all time and people will always remember me."

After years of praying that their dreams would come true, a group of woodsmen came upon the trees. When one came to the first tree he said, "This looks like a strong tree, I think I should be able to sell the wood to a carpenter," and he began cutting it down. The tree was happy, because he knew that the carpenter would turn him into a treasure chest.

At the second tree a woodsman said, "This looks like a strong tree, I should be able to sell it to the shipyard." The second tree was happy because he knew he was on his way to becoming a mighty ship.

When the woodsmen came upon the third tree, the tree was frightened because he knew that if they cut him down his dreams would not come true. One of the woodsmen said, "I don't feel anything special from my tree so I'll take this one," and he cut it down.

When the first tree arrived at the carpenter's, he was made into a feed box for animals. He was placed in a barn and filled with hay. This was not all he had prayed for.

The second tree was cut and made into a small fishing boat. His dreams of being a mighty ship and carrying kings had come to an end.

The third tree was cut into large pieces and left alone in the dark.

The years went by and the trees forgot about their dreams. Then one day, a man and a woman came to the barn. She gave birth and they placed the baby in the hay in the feed box that was made from the first tree. The man wished he could have made a crib for the baby, but this manger would have to do. The tree could feel the importance of this event and knew it had held the greatest treasure of all time.

Years later, a group of men got in the fishing boat made from the second tree. One of them was tired and went to sleep. While they were out on the water, a great storm arose and the tree didn't think it was strong enough to keep the men safe. The men woke the sleeping man and he stood and said "Peace be still," and the storm stopped. At this time, the tree knew that it had carried the King of Kings in its boat.

Finally, someone came and got the third tree. It was carried through the streets as the people mocked the man who was carrying it. When they came to a stop, the man was nailed to the tree and raised in the air to die at the top of a hill. When Sunday came, the tree came to realize that it was strong enough to stand at the top of the hill and be as close to God as was possible.

The moral of the story is that when things don't seem to be going your way, always know that God has a plan for you. Each of the trees got what they wanted, just not the way they had imagined.

We don't always know what God's plans are for us. We just know that His ways are not our ways, but His ways are always best.

"I am always content with what happens; for I know that what God chooses is better than what I choose."
- Epictetus

"Everyone has been made for some particular work, and the desire for that work has been put into his heart."
– Rumi

The Most Beautiful Heart

One day a young man was standing in the middle of the town proclaiming that he had the most beautiful heart in the whole valley. A large crowd gathered and they all admired his heart for it was perfect. There was not a mark or a flaw in it. Yes, they all agreed it truly was the most beautiful heart they had ever seen. The young man was very proud and boasted more loudly about his beautiful heart.

Suddenly, an old man appeared at the front of the crowd and said, "Why your heart is not nearly as beautiful as mine." The crowd and the young man looked at the old man's heart. It was beating strongly, but full of scars. It had places where pieces had been removed and other pieces put in, but they didn't fit quite right and there were several jagged edges. In fact, in some places there were deep gouges where whole pieces were missing.

The people stared. "How can he say his heart is more beautiful?" they thought.

The young man looked at the old man's heart and saw its state and laughed. "You must be joking," he said. "Compare your heart with mine, mine is perfect and yours is a mess of scars and tears."

"Yes," said the old man, "yours is perfect looking but I would never trade with you. You see, every scar represents a person to whom I have given my love—I tear out a piece of my heart and give it to them, and often they give me a piece of their heart which fits into the empty place in my heart, but because the pieces aren't exact, I have some rough edges, which I cherish because they remind me of the love we shared. Sometimes I have given pieces of my heart away and the other person hasn't returned a piece of his heart to me. These are the empty gouges—giving love is taking a chance. Although these gouges are painful, they stay open, reminding me of the love I have for these people too, and I hope someday they may return and fill the space I have waiting. So now do you see what true beauty is?"

The young man stood silently with tears running down his cheeks. He walked up to the old man, reached into his perfect young and beautiful heart, and ripped a piece out. He offered it to the old man with trembling hands. The old man took his offering, placed it in his heart and took a piece from his old scarred heart and placed it in the wound in the young man's heart. It fit, but not perfectly, as there were some jagged edges. The young man looked at his heart, not perfect anymore but more beautiful than ever, since love from the old man's heart flowed into his. They embraced and walked away side by side.

"Love in the heart wasn't put there to stay;
Love isn't love 'til it's given away."
- Author Unknown

God's Boxes

I have in my hands two boxes which God gave me to hold.

He said, "Put all your sorrows in the black, and all your joys in the gold."

I heeded His words, and in the two boxes both my joys and sorrows I stored.

But though the gold became heavier each day, the black was as light as before.

With curiosity, I opened the black; I wanted to find out why.

And I saw, in the base of the box, a hole, which my sorrows had fallen out by.

I showed the hole to God, and mused aloud, "I wonder where my sorrows could be."

He smiled a gentle smile at me, "My child, they're all here with me."

I asked, "God, why give me the boxes, why the gold and

the black with the hole?"

"My child, the gold is for you to count your blessings, the black is for you to let go."

"To be wronged is nothing unless you continue to remember it."
– Confucius

An Angel Is Watching Over You

There was this little girl sitting by herself in the park. Everyone passed by her and never stopped to see why she looked so sad. Dressed in a worn pink dress, barefoot and dirty, the girl just sat and watched the people go by. She never tried to speak; she never said a word. Many people passed but no one would stop.

The next day, I decided to go back to the park in curiosity to see if the girl would still be there. Yes, she was still there, right in the very spot she was yesterday, and still with the sad look in her eyes.

Today, I was to make my own move and walk over to the little girl. For as we all know, a park full of strange people is not a place for young children to play alone. As I got closer, I could see the back of the little girl's dress was obscenely shaped. I figured that was the reason people just passed by and made no effort to help. Deformities are a low blow to our society and heaven forbid if you make a step towards assisting someone who is different. As I walked closer, the little girl lowered her eyes slightly to avoid my intent stare. I could now see the obscene shape of her back more clearly. She was grotesquely shaped in a humped-over form. I smiled to let her know it was OK; I was there to help, to talk. I sat down beside her and opened with a simple hello. The little girl acted shocked and stammered a "hi," after a long stare into my eyes. I smiled and she shyly smiled back. We talked until darkness fell and the park was completely empty. I asked the girl why she was so sad.

The little girl looked at me and with a sad face said, "Because I'm different."

I immediately said, "That you are!" and smiled.

The little girl acted even sadder and said, "I know."

"Little girl," I said, "you remind me of an angel, sweet and innocent."

She looked at me and smiled. Slowly she got to her feet and said, "Really?"

"Yes, you're like a Guardian Angel sent to watch over all those people walking by."

She shook her head yes and smiled. With that, she spread her wings and said, "I'm *your* Guardian Angel," with a twinkle in her eye.

I was speechless; sure I was seeing things.

She said, "For once you thought of someone other than yourself. My job here is done."

I got to my feet and said, "Wait. So why did no one stop to help an angel?"

She looked at me and smiled, "You're the only one that could see me," and then she was gone.

And with that, my life changed dramatically.

So, when you think you're all you have, remember, your angel is always watching over you.

"Treat people as if they were what they ought to be and you help them to become what they are capable of becoming."
- Johann von Goethe

P.U.S.H.

A man was sleeping at night in his cabin when suddenly his room filled with light and the Savior appeared. The Lord told the man he had work for him to do and showed him a large rock in front of his cabin. The Lord explained that the man was to push against the rock with all his might. This the man did, day after day.

For many years, he toiled from sun up to sun down, his shoulders set squarely against the cold, massive surface of the unmoving rock, pushing with all his might. Each night the man returned to his cabin sore and worn out, feeling that his whole day had been spent in vain.

Seeing that the man was showing signs of discouragement, the Adversary decided to enter the picture by placing thoughts into the man's weary mind: "You have been pushing against that rock for a long time and it hasn't budged. Why kill yourself over this? You are never going to move it."

This gave the man the impression that the task was impossible and that he was a failure. These thoughts discouraged and disheartened the man. "Why kill myself over this?" he thought. "I'll put in my time, giving just the minimum effort and that will be good enough." And that is what he planned to do until one day he decided to make it a matter of prayer and take his troubled thoughts to the Lord.

"Lord," he said, "I have labored long and hard in your service, putting all my strength to do that which you have asked. Yet, after all this time, I have not even budged that rock by half a millimeter. What is wrong? Why am I failing?"

The Lord responded compassionately, "My friend, when I asked you to serve me and you accepted, I told you that your task was to push against the rock with all your strength, which you have done. Never once did I mention to you that I expected you to move it. Your task was to push. And now you come to me, with your strength spent, thinking you have failed. But is that really so? Look at yourself. Your arms are strong and muscled, your back sinewy and brown, your hands are calloused from constant pressure, and your legs have become massive and hard. Through opposition you have grown much and your abilities now surpass that which you used to have. Yet you haven't moved the rock. But your calling was to be obedient and to push and to exercise your faith and trust in My wisdom. This you have done. I, my friend, will now move the rock."

At times, when we hear a word from God, we tend to use our own intellect to decipher what He wants, when actually what God wants is just simple obedience and faith in Him. By all means, exercise the faith that moves mountains, but know that it is still God who moves the mountains.

Just P.U.S.H.
When everything seems to go wrong....P.U.S.H.
When the job gets you down....P.U.S.H.
When people don't react the way you think they
    should....P.U.S.H.
When your money is short and bills are due....P.U.S.H.
When you want to curse them out for whatever the
    reason....P.U.S.H.
When people just don't understand you....P.U.S.H.

P.U.S.H. — Pray Until Something Happens

"As soon as man rejects all visible help and human hope, and follows after God with faith and a pure heart, grace follows after him and reveals its power in help of various kinds."
- Isaac of Syria

Hang On to Each Other

Too often we feel alone. But there is always someone ready to take our hand. There is a beautiful story of an overworked nurse who escorted a tired, young man to her patient's bedside. Leaning over and speaking loudly to the elder patient, she said, "Your son is here." With great effort, his unfocussed eyes opened, then flickered shut again. The young man squeezed his aged hand in his hand and sat beside the bed. Throughout the night he sat there, holding the old man's hand and whispering words of comfort.

By morning's light, the patient had died. In moments, hospital staff swarmed into the room to turn off machines and remove needles. The nurse stepped over to the young man's side and began to offer sympathy, but he interrupted her.

"Who was that man?" he asked.

The startled nurse replied, "I thought he was your father!"

"No, he was not my father," he answered. "I never saw him before in my life."

"Then, why didn't you say something when I took you to him?"

"I realized he needed his son and his son wasn't here," the man explained. "And since he was too sick to recognize that I was not his son, I knew he needed me."

Mother Teresa used to remind us that nobody should have to die alone. Likewise, nobody should have to grieve alone or cry alone, or laugh alone or celebrate alone. We are made to travel life's journey hand in hand. There is someone ready to grasp your hand today. And someone is hoping you will take theirs.

"I wasn't there that morning when my father passed away...I didn't get to tell him all the things I had to say. I just wish I could have told him in the living years."
- Mike & The Mechanics – *The Living Years*

An Angel to Watch Over You

Once upon a time, there was a child ready to be born, so one day he asked God, "They tell me you're sending me to Earth tomorrow, but how am I going to live there being so small and helpless?"

God said, "Among the many angels, I chose one for you. She will be waiting for you and will take care of you."

"But tell me, here in Heaven I don't do anything but sing and smile. That's enough for me to be happy."

"Your angel will sing for you and will smile for you every day. And you will feel your angel's love and be happy."

"And how am I going to be able to understand when people talk to me if I don't understand the language they speak?"

"Your angel will tell you the most beautiful and sweet words you will ever hear and with much patience and care, your angel will teach you how to speak."

"And what am I going to do when I want to talk to you?"

"Your angel will place your hands together and will teach you how to pray."

"I've heard that on Earth there are bad men. Who will protect me?"

"Your angel will defend you even when it means risking her life."

"But I will always be sad because I will not see you anymore."

"Your angel will always talk to you about Me and will teach you the way for you to come back to Me even though I will always be next to you."

At that moment there was much peace in Heaven. But voices from Earth could already be heard and the child in a hurry asked softly, "Oh God, if I'm about to leave now, please tell me my angel's name."

"Your angel's name is of no importance. You will simply call her mommy."

"Everyone entrusted with a mission is an angel....All forces that reside in the body are angels."
- Maimonides

The Other Side

When I was a little boy, my mother used to embroider a great deal. I would sit at her knee and look up from the floor and ask what she was doing. She informed me that she was embroidering. From the underside, I watched her work within the boundaries of the little round hoop she held in her hand. I once complained to her that it sure looked messy from where I sat. She smiled at me, looked down and gently said, "My son, you go about your playing for a while and when I am finished with my embroidering, I will put you on my knee and let you see it from my side."

I wondered why she was using some dark threads along with the bright ones and why they seemed so jumbled from my view. A few minutes passed and then I heard Mother's voice say, "Son, come and sit on my knee." This I did, only to be surprised and thrilled to see a beautiful flower. I could not believe it because from underneath it had looked so messy. Then Mother said to me, "My son, from underneath it did look messy and jumbled, but you did not realize that there was a pre-drawn plan on the top. It was a design and I was only following it. Now look at it from my side and you will see what I was doing."

Many times through the years, I have looked up to God and asked, "Father, what are You doing?"

He has answered, "I am embroidering your life."

I say, "But it looks like a mess to me. It seems so jumbled. The threads seem so dark. Why can't they all be bright?"

The Father seems to tell me, "My child, you go about your business of doing My business, and one day I will bring you to Heaven and put you on My knee and you will see the plan from My side."

"Life and death are one thread, the same line viewed from different sides."
- Lao-tzu

From Illusion to Reality

— Part 5—

Ask Andrew

It's been said that the only dumb question is the one that's never asked. For those who may have questions but either were afraid to ask or didn't know where to get a reliable answer, I've provided a deeper viewpoint to some of life's most common questions that deal with every part of life.

Dear Andrew…How do you incorporate spirituality into everyday life?…C.F., WPB, FL

Most people lead very busy lives. They get caught up in the drama that is their life and usually take time out on Saturday, Sunday or maybe just the important holidays to remember God. Being spiritual is not remembering God during the time-outs, but actually incorporating Him into everyday life, in all your actions. One of our reasons for being here is to learn how to incorporate spirituality into our everyday lives. In fact, every challenge we go through is actually an opportunity for us to demonstrate our inner spirit. At every moment, we are given a choice. We can travel the highest path and do what is "right" or we can take a path that may not represent our highest good. Each choice brings about corresponding consequences. What we want to do before every choice is ask ourselves, *"Is this for my highest good?"* or *"What would the spirit in me do?"* Obviously this is not going to happen overnight. Every change in habit requires time. Next time you are in a situation that requires you to *re-act* (act as you've acted before), ask yourself those questions and you'll probably find a new way to act. Amazingly enough, you will probably notice things will start going your way.

Dear Andrew…With so many religions out there, how do you know which one is "right?" And if one is "right" does that mean that the others are "wrong?"… J.M., Norwalk, CT

Let's first understand that religion is man's best attempt to interpret the "Word of God." All the teachings of Jesus, Moses, Buddha and Mohammed have been retold by many men. When that happens, the teachings pass through a filter – the human mind. When something passes through a filter, it changes the original product, or message.

Most religions have similar core beliefs. They believe in one All Powerful, All Loving, Supreme Being – or God. Where they differ is in the customs, rules or restrictions that are added and interpreted as being the "Word of God."

I cannot tell you what is "right." That is for each one of you to decide. One way to help you decide what is best for you is by listening to what you are *feeling*. Feelings reside in your soul and your soul is part of God in you. The true "Word of God" should promote love, not hatred; freedom, not restrictions; harmony, not separation; equality, not competition. If you follow those guidelines, you will be led closer to the true "Word of God."

Dear Andrew…I'm going through a lot of pain in my life, and can't figure out the lesson. I feel like I've learned all the lessons. Please help!…J.H., WPB, FL

When you finally learn all of the lessons you are here to learn in this lifetime, your mission will be complete and you will no longer need to reside in this vehicle you call "your body." As long as you are still here, you have more lessons to learn. A bit of advice for you…When you say that you've learned all of life's lessons, you are closing yourself to the possibility of learning more. Socrates was one of the wisest men of all because he *knew* that he knew nothing. Therefore, he was always ready, willing and able to learn more. Do not try to figure this out with your mind. The solution is not of the mind, but of the spirit. Just ask God (or your spirit) to show you the way and then watch for the answers to appear. I guarantee that the answers will appear, but I cannot guarantee that you will recognize them when they do. Every time you experience deep pain, you are not connected to your source and thus feel lost, awaiting direction and solutions. Know that you are not alone and that you are feeling these feelings because you haven't identified the TRUE lesson. You are still, on a subconscious level, resisting them, thus causing pain. The pain you are going through is an illusion; it only exists in your mind. When you figure this out, the pain will disappear. The most important step is to acquire the DESIRE to know the TRUTH. The pain is being used to bring about your desire. Remember, not a desire of the mind, but a deep desire of the soul to know the TRUTH and let the TRUTH be revealed to you. When you have the desire then you will be able to see the signs, which will lead you out of the forest where you are temporarily lost. Keep going my friend. Everything will be OK. God never gives us more than we can handle.

Dear Andrew...If you were sending your child out into the world, what would be the three most important things you would tell him?... M, WPB, FL

The three most valuable things I could prepare my child with would be as follows:

1) *Treat others as you want to be treated.*

This is one of the most important Universal Laws to remember. Once you realize this and learn how to master it, you will be able to control how people treat you. You can only do that by monitoring how you treat others. If society figured this one out and mastered it, we would live in our own "Heaven on Earth," with no war, starvation or crime.

2) *There are no mistakes, only lessons.*
   Once you realize that everything you go through is designed to teach you something and help you evolve, you will embrace every challenge for what it truly is, an opportunity to grow. You will live in a world where you never get upset because you realize that nothing is "bad," and you will find out what it is trying to teach you. This will allow you to evolve much more quickly and experience a life that most people never thought possible.

3) *Find out your "true" reason for being here, and follow it.*
   We all have a reason for being here but most people haven't figured it out yet. The reason is because we keep following what our brains tell us. The answer cannot be found with the brain. Our spirit knows why we are really here and when we get in touch with our spirit, it will start leading us towards our "true" mission. First, you need to desire to know your "true" mission, then you need the awareness to identify it. And last, you need the courage to follow the path that it leads you to.

Dear Andrew...I am at the point in my spiritual path that I'd like to demonstrate "SURRENDER." I'm having trouble with this one. Any tips?...M.S., WPB, FL

First we must understand that our spirit knows what is "best" for us. The only way we can truly be led by our spirit to what is for our highest good is if we completely let go of our plan for what's best. In other words, we must surrender our plan for our spirit's plan. That requires absolute faith.

I'll use an example we can all relate to. If a father asks his little child to jump into his arms and the child is worried that his father won't catch him, the child will not jump. In order

Ask Andrew

for the child to jump, he must have absolute faith (complete trust) that his father will catch him. Only then will he jump, which requires complete surrender to his father. We know that every loving father will always catch his child when he jumps.

Keeping with the father—child analogy, if your Father (God or Spirit) asked His child (you) to jump into his arms (surrender), do you think he would let you fall? Of course not, the loving Father will always catch His child.

The key to complete surrender is having absolute faith. Everybody thinks they have faith, and they all do, to a certain extent, but your faith must be stretched. That requires you to experience certain situations that bring up a fear response and replace it with faith, or a trusting response. Your brain may not understand that it's all okay but just trust that everything will be all right. Your Father will not let you fall.

Dear Andrew...What is your take on the Bible?...P.K., Bayside, NY

Many people think that the Bible represents the one and only "Word of God" but God has been speaking to man long before and long after the Bible was written. This book represents one of many divinely inspired works that are designed to help humanity understand spiritual truths. Other divinely inspired works that can unlock the understanding of higher truths include the Koran, the Kabbalah, the Bhagavad Gita and the Tao Te Ching. We have to remember that each book was inspired by God, but written by man. The word inspired means "in-spirit" which means that the person writing the book was acting as a channel for Spirit. Everything that came through that writer came through his mind, which acted as a filter. As you know, a filter changes something from its original form. I believe it is important to understand that so as not to be attached to the belief that certain words or writings are the *only* "true words of God."

The Bible is a book that was designed to be understood on

273

many levels. The deeper it is understood, the greater the treasure that is received. When looked at on the deepest level, you will realize that it is a guide to unlocking the keys to finding inner peace, to creating a life that is truly *"Heaven on Earth,"* and to re-union with our Source, or what many people call "Heaven." For that reason alone, it is one of the greatest books ever written.

Dear Andrew...Is it possible to work towards financial freedom without sacrificing one's personal life?...D.F., WPB, FL

Most people think that in order to achieve success in life, you must work harder and longer than everyone else. Well, that's usually not the case. The most successful people in the world know that *"working smart, not hard"* can get you a lot further. *"Working smart"* can actually be taken to the next level when you understand how the universe works and by applying those powerful principles to your everyday life. I'm sure everyone would love to know how it all *really* works, but most people will not bother to learn it, or they think they know it all already. That will put you on the fast track to a life of *hard work until retirement*.

I define financial freedom as the ability to do *what* you want, *when* you want. If you can't do what you want because you have to go to work, that means you're not doing what you are supposed to be doing in your life. Most people are stuck in jobs they don't like and their excuse is that they have to pay the bills or support a family. They never bothered finding out what was possible for them and got stuck in a routine they could never get out of.

I recommend taking the steps now, which will provide that freedom you're searching for, such as studying and _applying_ those Universal Principles. It is a process that takes time, but you are going to be here for the rest of your life anyway so you might as well make it as productive and pleasurable as you can.

Dear Andrew...I am a homeless person and feel that people judge me because of the way I look. I would like to be treated like a person. What do you think?...M.S., WPB, FL

Unfortunately, we still live in a time when people judge other people by their appearances. They do not understand that we are all spirits in human form. Some of us have just chosen a different form for this lifetime. When we find ourselves getting upset at being judged by our appearance, we must practice detachment and forgiveness. Those are two very powerful spiritual principles that can provide us with a tremendous amount of freedom when understood and applied properly. So next time, try that. It may not stop them from judging you, but YOU will feel a lot better. Remember, you cannot control what people say or do, you can only control how you feel about what people say or do.

Dear Andrew...My son is going through adolescence and giving me problems. I'm losing my patience and my temper. I'm in desperate need to know what to do...Anonymous, WPB, FL

Your son is going through what we all go through, the transformation of child into adult. He is at that difficult age when he wants to learn to make his own decisions, while you still feel you should. When you both want to exercise your control and have it your way, that will always lead to conflict. Sometimes parents have a difficult time letting go and allowing their children to grow up. (This is actually a common problem for parents and children, no matter how old they are.) When he expects resistance from you, he comes to you with a combatative attitude. If you remove the resistance, his attitude will change. We don't want to make anyone our enemy; we always want them to be an ally. If you trust your son, I would recommend backing off a bit and allowing him to make his own decisions. You'll probably be surprised at how capable he is of handling himself.

Dear Andrew...I've run across this quote before which says, "When we recognize that we create our own karma and are, therefore, responsible for our own experience, both good and bad, doesn't this penetrating insight free us from resentment and frustration, instilling a sense of freedom and responsibility?" No it doesn't. I am, in fact, drowning in a sea of resentment and frustration! At best, I'm thrashing around hoping karma will send me a lifeline. What do you think?...H.M.

You can throw yourself your own lifeline once you realize that as long as you keep sending out feelings of resentment and frustration, you will attract negative scenarios into your life. That's like jumping off a building and getting upset every time you hit the ground and hurt yourself. The Law of Gravity is ALWAYS in effect and you must be aware how it works so you can use it to your advantage. The Law of Attraction is ALWAYS in effect and the way it works is whatever thought and feeling you send out is ALWAYS attracting a corresponding consequence into your reality (Cause and Effect). In other words, when you send out a positive feeling, you are attracting what you desire, when you send out a negative feeling, you are attracting what you do not desire. Resentment and frustration are negative feelings, therefore, you are attracting situations and events into your life that you do not desire, or that you would consider "BAD." The reason why this frees us is because once we realize HOW we unconsciously create both "GOOD" and "BAD" into our lives, we can spend more time focusing on consciously creating "GOOD." I hope this helps clarify it a little more.

Dear Andrew…Whenever I try to manifest something I see it come into view but then it seems that I always push it away. What can I do to have it show up completely?…M.K., Boca Raton., FL

That is actually very common. Most people attract something to where they can see it in the distance because they have been putting out the proper feelings, but once they see it, they try to pull it in too fast and change their feelings to one of need or impatience and end up pushing it away. In other words, it's the *"allowing"* that gives us trouble. Remember, to attract something into your life, you must send out positive feelings so you can attract what you desire. When you can see it in the distance, it's still an illusion and you can't experience it yet. You must remain patient and <u>allow</u> it to get from the point you can *see* it to the point you can *touch* it. Patience is more important than you think because it is the final piece to the puzzle of creating what you desire.

Dear Andrew…My fiancée and I have been engaged for about a year and we have less than a year to go until the wedding. I'm writing because I have a serious problem with her "so-called" religion. I'm a devout Christian, and am taught "Jesus is the way." She considers herself a Wiccan. I love this woman, without a doubt, but I have such a hard time accepting this part of her life. Could you please share some insight?…Anonymous

Many of the problems we face today are because we find ways to label ourselves, which separates us instead of allowing us to acknowledge that we are ALL ONE. We are ALL HUMAN BEINGS, some may be different color, some may have different beliefs. If we can see through the differences, we will see that we truly are all the same. Jesus Christ taught that we should accept everyone as our "brother." This would be a good time to follow His advice, and to follow the love that you feel. That love is your spirit's way of telling you to head in that direction. The negative feelings you feel is spirit's way of telling you NOT to listen to the voice that is labeling and judging someone to be different from you and to change the direction of your thoughts.

Dear Andrew...I'm trying to raise some money to study abroad. I've considered asking friends and family to help me out, but I think I will still come up short. Any advice on how to come up with the rest?...T.M., WPB, FL

The best help I can give is to show you how you can access what is available to all of us. There's an old saying that says, *"Give a man a fish, he eats for a day; teach a man to fish, he eats for a lifetime."* I will show you how you can get what you want, whenever you want.

First, you must understand that Spirit will do whatever you ask, if it's for your highest good. Think of it as your partner, He does His work on His side; you do your work on your side. Most of us NEVER call on our partner to help and He's just sitting there waiting to be asked. So let Him know what you want and need and ask Him for help and then thank Him as if it's done. It is done; it just hasn't shown up in your life yet. Then watch as the synchronistic events take place that lead you to what you want. It's an amazing process that works, if we utilize it properly. It's very important to be patient after you send out your request. Impatience keeps what you're searching for away. Patience shows faith, which brings it to you.

This process will work if you apply it to ANY situation. If you're looking to change jobs, looking to buy (or sell) the right car or home, looking for something you've lost, trying to get out of a medical, financial or legal challenge, or simply want guidance as to what direction to take in your life, you can do a much better job with your partner than by yourself.

Dear Andrew...What is your take on divorce? The Bible says, "God says He hates divorce."...J.S., WPB, FL

First of all, you must remember that the passage you're referring to was not written by God, but by a man who was inspired by God. That message came through his filter, or mind, and was tainted by his beliefs on the subject. Over the long period of time it took to write the Bible, man's view of God changed from an angry God to a loving God. When you understand that God is "unconditional love" you'll realize there are no conditions to that love. God does not "hate" anything, therefore, he cannot hate divorce. "Hate" is a very human emotion and we should not project that onto God. Of course if we make a decision as important as that, we should try everything in our power to make it work. Sometimes, though, we marry the person who was only supposed to be a temporary lesson in our lives, and in cases like that, it's up to us to realize we must move on. God would not want us to spend our whole life in "fifth grade" just because we "got married" because we will never get the lesson that "sixth grade" provides.

Dear Andrew...I continue to try to be a giver to others, but seem to get taken advantage of in the end. What is wrong with me?...O.M.

Nothing is *wrong* with you, it's just that there's something you're not aware of yet. Nobody can take advantage of us without our permission. We must learn to put up a fair boundary that should be respected. Giving is a beautiful thing, when it's done from love (not fear or insecurity) and it should produce a wonderful feeling. When our giving produces a feeling of being taken advantage of, it means our boundaries have been compromised. The only reason that happens is because, at that moment, we fear hurting someone else's feelings. The lesson, therefore, is for us. We must learn to be strong, yet fair, in order to find a happy balance that leaves everyone feeling good.

Understand, that you'll keep repeating the lesson until you've learned it, and you'll know you've learned it when you've changed your actions. So be prepared to be put in the same situation again, and know that you must put up that boundary and hold onto your own power.

Dear Andrew... You write that pain can be an illusion. What about those situations that are completely out of our control? My father was murdered two years ago and to this day I still feel the pain. It's not easy to LET GO of someone you loved so dearly.... E.S., WPB, FL

The topic you discuss is never easy but is one that must be faced. The loss of a loved one, especially when it's in a way that can be as shocking as yours was, is never easy and painless. It's important and proper to feel the emotions that come up in a time like that. Those emotions are felt very deeply and can definitely be thought of as painful. We should feel them and then let them go and move on with the lessons of life. It's when we hold on to those emotions that the unnecessary pain comes in. *Suffering is simply the difference between what is and what we want it to be.* Many times, we don't understand what the death of a loved one represents from the bigger perspective. From our limited point of view, we feel hurt, abandoned, violated, wronged, confused, all which lead to extreme pain. We must try to see things from the greater perspective and then things begin to become clear. It has been my experience that when we do, we start to realize that there is a plan for everything and God really is in control, and that is a wonderful feeling. We know that God (Spirit) is unlimited and we (humans) are limited, so we must strive to access the unlimited view of Spirit in order to make sense of things. When we do, we start to live a life where everything unfolds as it's supposed to and since it now makes more sense to us, we don't resist it; therefore, we have less pain in our lives.

Dear Andrew…It seems that my best friend and I have been fighting a lot lately. How can I get this cycle to stop?…Anonymous

You must understand that within every relationship, there is a lesson to be learned for BOTH people that the other one is able to provide. Your friend is here to teach you more about the areas *you* need to work on and you're here to help your friend learn more about what *she* needs to work on. This does not happen directly, but rather indirectly. The other person brings out parts in us that upset us or cause resistance in our lives and, at that moment, we MUST look at OURSELVES and ask, *"What am I supposed to be learning about ME here? Do I need to learn to be more loving, patient, non-judgmental, honest, tolerant, secure, open and communicative, etc."*

You both have issues you need to work on that the other one is helping bring to the surface. Unfortunately, as is common with most everyone, we don't look at our lessons; we only look at the other one's. My advice is that when you speak to each other, you make a commitment to help each other work on your own issues and allow each other a safe space to "screw up" and talk about how the other person may be bugging you. When we fear the opinion others have of us, ones that may be right, we do not allow ourselves to get to that space that is required to heal those areas we need to heal within ourselves.

Dear Andrew...A friend of mine is abusing drugs and it's tearing his family apart. His mother is totally distraught and feels like a complete failure. Any words of advice?...Anonymous

Whether we want to believe it or not, EVERYTHING has a divine plan behind it. This is no exception. Spirit is always trying to get our attention. It wants us to include It in our lives more than we have been and to start applying spiritual principles into our everyday lives but we always think we know everything so we are usually closed to It. If we don't hear Its call at first, It will start to get a little louder until It's forced to "scream" at us. The pain and frustration is what allows us to open up to Spirit.

This family is being asked to allow these principles into their lives in a greater way and they have not been listening so the universe is using their son to get their attention.

All things on the physical plane (outer) have their source in the plane of Spirit (inner). That is where they must be healed. The only way to heal an outer condition is to heal it on the inner level. People can spend years trying every human option their brains can think of and they usually will before they allow a spiritual solution to be implemented. But we all have the option of saving all that time and implementing them NOW. When we raise our consciousness, eventually these challenges start to dissolve on their own and shed away. So we must focus on raising our consciousness and everything else will follow.

Dear Andrew...I recently had a yearlong relationship falter. The reasoning was that financial security was more important than love. I believe love is the foundation that financial security will rest upon. How do you move forward and let go of someone that I feel in my heart is the one for me?...R

Letting go of a loved one and moving on from a relationship can be difficult, especially when we feel that person was "the one." So many times we think we've met "*the* one" we're supposed to be with forever. Most of the time, though, that's not the case. That person is the "*one*" but that just means he/she is the one person who's supposed to be in our lives at THIS moment, in order to take us to our next level of evolution, not necessarily forever. Every relationship is in our lives to help us grow. The closest relationships are the ones that help us to grow the most. They allow us to reach into the deepest parts of ourselves and see who we really are. They bring out parts of us that we never knew existed, because those are the parts that need to be faced and healed, not ignored, like most of us do. When we've gotten all we're supposed to from the relationship, it will end and the individuals will move on to the next "one" for the next lesson. When we hold on to our idea of who that person was, thinking that we were supposed to be with them forever, we bring pain into our lives. If we can bless that person for playing his/her part in our lives and helping us grow, we can ease the pain and allow both of us to move on to the next part of our journey.

Dear Andrew…I'm having a problem with something you wrote in a past issue about relationships and when they end. I do agree that every relationship is in our lives to help us grow but I believe that we need to do everything possible, especially in a marriage, before we call it quits. Sometimes more growth is acquired when we stay and work through the things that are giving us the most trouble. Thanks for listening…N.T., Springfield, MA

I agree with your position 100%. I do not believe we should run at the first sign of trouble and think that something better will come along. That is just avoiding the lesson at hand. I believe we should do our best to try to communicate and work the problem out, but after we've done all we can, we must be aware of the signs when they tell us it's time to move on. Not every relationship is meant to be in our lives on a permanent basis. Some people are only supposed to be in our lives for certain reasons and when those reasons have been fulfilled, their job is done and they will either leave our lives or the relationship will change forms.

Too many times, people are so attached to what they want that they are unable to recognize the guidance Spirit is giving them. When we detach from our will and surrender to God's will, we then open up to the guidance that will tell us if we should remain in the relationship or if it has served its purpose in our lives. The universe knows where we're at and what lessons we need by the choices we make. There is no "right" or "wrong" choice. Whatever choice we make brings upon the proper lesson for us.

Dear Andrew...It seems that I have a recurring pattern with the same type of people entering my life. They all seem to have an issue with anger. I've always had an issue with anger, as well. What's the connection?...A.P., WPB, FL

The people that show up in our lives are there to help us learn more about *ourselves*. When a pattern keeps recurring and the same type of people keep showing up in our lives, the universe is telling us what part of ourselves we need to work on. Those people are mirrors to help us look at ourselves more closely. In this case, you say that you've always had an issue with anger so the universe keeps bringing people with anger issues into your life so you can see how it feels to be someone on the receiving end of that anger and realize that you must change that area of your life. You must also remember that *like attracts like,* in other words, we attract people into our lives who are of the same "vibration," or who think and act like we do.

The only way to have people with anger issues stop showing up in your life is for you to heal this issue and stop being angry. If you keep neglecting the issue at hand, the universe will get "louder" and the situations will get worse until you finally change your behavior.

Dear Andrew...It's been said that it's extremely difficult for a "rich man to get into heaven." Is it more "spiritual" to not have money? ...Doc, WPB, FL

Money is just energy; it's not "good" or "bad." It's how it's used that is the key. It's the same with nuclear energy; it can be used to power a city (good) or it can be used to destroy a city (bad). The energy itself is neutral; it's the intentions of the people behind the energy that determine its contribution to society. Money was given to us to do many things. Some people use it to do good things and some to do bad things. Many people also use money for their benefit alone. I believe that it's not a contest to see who can acquire the most. I feel people who have been blessed with the ability to attract abundance in their lives should use some of it to enhance the lives of others. Just as electricity is an energy that we use while we're taking up space on this planet and should be used to make ALL life more comfortable, money is another form of energy that should be used in that manner. Imagine if everybody said, *"What can I do with some of my money to help?"* Then money would be pretty spiritual. You can either have a "taker" mentality or a "giver" mentality.

The reason why it's "difficult for a rich man to get into heaven" is because money can be a tremendous distraction from our spiritual path. You must remember that our main reason for being here is to give our spirit a chance to evolve and many times, money, or better yet, the things money can buy, keep our focus off of the deepest spiritual matters and squarely on physical and material matters. Remember, the only thing you take with you when you die is your spirit and the lessons it has learned; you don't take the money or material possessions with you. Allow money to help make your life and the lives of others more comfortable while you're here on Earth, but always keep it in its proper perspective; in other words, don't make it your God. That's what the commandment *"You will have no other Gods before Me"* really means. If you've made money (or your job, or power, or physical pleasures such as sex, drugs or alcohol for that matter) your God, then it will be difficult to "get into heaven." Remember your Source and that everything (including money) comes from that Source. Knowing that, put your Source first.

Dear Andrew…I have a sister who has gone through some difficult challenges but now carries around a great deal of anger towards everyone, including me and treats me like a doormat. Every Christmas she really gets on my case and it ruins my holiday. I've always tried sending her love, but this past time, I decided to give her what she's been giving me and let it out in a nasty argument with her. Now, my Mom is taking her side and is angry with me. What should I do? … from an Angel in Pain

This is one of the major tests you and your sister signed up for before you came down here (Earth). The game is played best when we forget this, but the object is to remember it and walk through the anger and hatred. It's not guaranteed and you certainly cannot control what she does but you can and you must control how you act towards her. You need to step back and see through the illusion to her true essence and know that she doesn't remember the agreement that was made. That's why she's so angry. Send her love for playing her role so wonderfully and from a distance, keep sending her love and compassion for what she's going through. You saw the consequences (karma) you received from responding to her with anger. I know it's not easy but the universe is perfect and will always balance itself (anger out = anger back, i.e. your Mom towards you). It has gotten to the point where you're expecting her to act a certain way before you see her around Christmas and of course, you're proven right. Well, that's because you're creating that by expecting it and feeling it like it's happening before it happens. You need to visualize her feeling good and being at peace and FEEL it as if it's real. If you keep thinking, *"There's no way this is going to happen,"* you'll end up being right. When the situation seems real in your visualization, it will become real in your reality. It will take time to get your visualization vibration to where you want it but remember, whatever is showing up in your life is there because that's what is vibrationally matching your vibration. Change the vibe you're offering and you will change what shows up. IT IS LAW!

I recently received an email about prayer in school from someone who thought it was wrong that prayer was not allowed in school. The e-mail went on to give a prayer that they felt was all right to share before a high school football game. In the prayer the person said, "...*praise and thank God, and ask Him in the name of Jesus...*"

Here was my response:

Written in the piece is the challenge. He says to pray to God "*in the name of Jesus*" and that's why there is a problem. This country is unique in that it's built on people from many cultures. Therefore, respecting one's beliefs and cultures is extremely important if we are to live along side each other in peace. How can we tell everyone in school to pray to Jesus when it's not part of their belief structure? That's why we have such a problem in this country allowing prayer in school, whose God do we pray to? I'm not taking sides here; I'm just trying to point out why there is a problem. Not allowing prayer in school will not keep people from praying to Jesus, or whomever they pray to, on their own time. Everyone should be concerned about their own beliefs and being the best "Christian, Jew, Muslim, or whatever" they are and not be so concerned with making sure everyone follows their God. I say "*Live, Love and Allow.*"

As long as one group of people thinks their God is better there will be a problem. I understand your strong belief in Jesus and I think it's great that you believe so strongly but we must allow everyone their own beliefs and respect their choices, as well. Instead of saying "*our God is better, or the only way,*" let's just say "*our God is a different way*" and allow everyone their right to choose their way. This type of thinking will bring peace on Earth very quickly. The other way hasn't worked very well in the past few thousand years and, in fact, is the biggest reason for killing in the history of mankind. Choices like these define humanity. I choose peace. How about you?

Closing Thoughts

The key to understanding anything lies in KNOWING it on an inner level. In other words, *"What does your inner voice say?"* You can use another person's words and ideas as a guide but you must formulate your own opinion. Most people don't ever take the time to think about things and figure out what it means to them. They just follow and recite what other people do and say.

Here are a few quotes that have made me think and reach the "well of wisdom" that lies inside all of us. Most people have never tapped into that "well" but when you do, you will be amazed at what lies buried inside. *I ask that you take a few minutes and ponder what each quote means to you*. Do not try to think of the meaning on the surface, dig a little deeper. Remember, that is where the treasures lie.

*"Knowing others is intelligence,
knowing oneself is true wisdom.
Mastering others is strength,
mastering yourself is true power."*

<u>Justice:</u> *when you get what you deserve.*
<u>Mercy:</u> *when you don't get what you deserve.*
<u>Grace:</u> *when you get what you don't deserve.*

*"When one door closes, another opens but often we look
so long at the closed door that we don't see the one which
has opened for us."*

*"If you walk through all the light there is and into the
darkness of the unknown – one of two things will happen;
there will be something solid on which to stand or you will
be taught how to fly."*

It is my wish that this guide has provided
you with the wings to fly and find the
treasure we're all searching for.

~ Andrew Moss
Human Being

...the journey continues... Spring 2003...

Would you like to get PAID for recommending this book?

When you recommend a movie, a book or a restaurant to a friend, are you ever compensated for it? The movie studio, publisher or restaurant obviously received a profit from your recommendation but, unfortunately, none of it was shared with you.

In an effort to further my idea of *"Give Back by Giving Forward,"* I would like to give back to you whenever someone buys my book because of your recommendation. I will give you 20% of the purchase price ($5.00) every time you tell someone about the book and they buy it.

How can I do this?

I've decided to market this book through a unique marketing method called *Referral Marketing.* Instead of selling the book at major bookstores and paying huge corporations the 20% they generally charge, I've decided to give that money back to the people who recommend the book. I feel the big corporations have enough money, so I'd rather see the money redistributed to the people who have been enjoying the book and recommending it to others.

Raise Money for Charities, Alumni Groups, Corporations, Associations and Organizations

I call it *"Raising Money While Raising Consciousness."* You can raise money for your organization by recommending my book to members. The organization will receive 20% of all book purchases. I will handle all of the shipping and administrative details. All the organization does is recommend the book and receive a check. *(For more information, see the following page)*

It's Easy

To start receiving your referral fees for yourself or your organization, all you have to do is sign up (for *Free*) either by:

1. Printing or typing your name, Social Security number, phone number, address where you'd like your checks sent to - and mailing it to: From Illusion to Reality, Get Paid for Sharing Dept., 6901 W. Okeechobee Blvd., #D-5/334, West Palm Beach, FL 33411
2. Online at www.fromillusiontoreality.com and *click on: Get Paid for Sharing,* or
3. By phone, by calling toll free: (866) 4-REAL99 (473-2599) and tell us you'd like to register to receive your referral fees.

You will be given an Affiliate ID Number, which will track all of your referral fees. After that, all you do is recommend the book and give them your Affiliate ID Number to use when they buy the book and 20% ($5.00) will be credited to your account. Checks will be sent out once a month.

So let's help each other by sharing this book with those you care about and at the same time, raise some extra money for yourself or your organization.

Raising Money
While Raising Consciousness

As we move forward into the new millennium, we are faced with many challenges. We must deal with war, disease, poverty, crime, drug addiction, child abuse and so many other challenges that rip into our hearts as we become aware of how prevalent they are in today's society. The citizens of this planet have made tremendous efforts to do something about these challenges, as charitable organizations around the world have been formed to lessen the effect each one has on our brothers and sisters across the globe. Although each organization does tremendous work, they are only dealing with the *"effect."* In order to truly accomplish their goal, though, they must work at the *"source"* of the problem. And that *"source"* is our *consciousness*. Our "outer" world is created by our "inner" consciousness, therefore, trying to heal the effects without raising our consciousness will NEVER work and that is <u>guaranteed</u>.

In an effort to realize true and lasting results and move the planet to what deep down inside everyone knows we are capable of experiencing, I am creating a program called *"Raising Money While Raising Consciousness."* I will be aligning with different charities around the world and donating 20% of the sales from this book to each organization that promotes it. What this does is raise additional money for the organization to work on the "effect" that it chooses, while at the same time, work at the "source" of all who read the book by raising their consciousness. The book is a practical guide that will teach everyone how things *really* work and how to create the lives we've always dreamed of. As society starts becoming aware of these principles and begins to apply them into everyday life, the world will start to experience the changes we all have been waiting for.

This book will not be sold in bookstores, only online and over the phone using a toll-free number. This will allow the extra money to be redirected to charities across the world. In addition, each year, I will introduce a new product, such as Book 2, Book 3, and a CD music line, which will add to the revenues being generated, which in turn gives back 20% to the charities.

If you would like a portion of the millions of dollars that will be generated, contact the *From Illusion to Reality Foundation* at (866) 4-REAL-99 (473-2599) to discuss how we can help fund your mission.

About the Artist

Jacqueline Ripstein is an International artist, self-made, and has participated in more than 300 art shows around the world. She is the creator of the Invisible Art & Light Technique© & pat., and it is her legacy to humanity. She is bringing art to a new dimension, as guidance and healing in the 21st century. The Invisible Art & Light Technique uses vibrations that are 1/8th above what our eyes can see and, like Mozart's music, it embodies new forms of expressions that project images and higher vibrations of the here-after and all that exists in the Higher planes.

This revolutionary technique uses the ultraviolet color that is invisible to the eye under normal light. When viewed under a black light, though, an image is revealed and the viewer experiences a breakthrough to a new path and a new consciousness. The violet color is the highest vibration of all colors; it is the color of the seekers. Divine energy can more easily be manifested through the ultraviolet images. When the viewer receives this energy, his inner-self automatically awakens and his vibration is raised; breaking the barriers of the mind and tearing down the walls of fears accumulated over time. A balanced state begins to appear in the body, mind and spirit and is the beginning of the process of *"bringing Heaven to Earth."* Jacqueline's art is the union of the Scientific, Material and Spiritual worlds; the union between the Body and the Soul; the union of Man with God.

The cover of this book is a piece called *"The Sacred Journey"* (as seen under a black light), which reveals the images of the Divine at work in our lives as we take this sacred journey *from illusion to reality.* What you are seeing is the hidden reality that we are still unaware of but are slowly waking up to. As you can see, we have help all around us on this journey but it's up to us to allow that help to be used in our lives on a daily basis.

Each of Jacqueline's paintings is a message she receives from the Divine that she is communicating to humanity. Each painting carries with it a written essence that must be shared, as well. The following is the essence accompanying the painting called *"The Sacred Journey."*

A path for mankind.
A path for growing.
The overcoming of Myths and Fears.
A new age where we are called on to explore into the realm of Divine ideas.
A breakthrough to a new path and new consciousness.
Others have crossed the bridge.
Awaken as a child again, your intuitive power.
Let the spiritual world help you! They love you! We love you!
In the path of love, we have the whole of eternity for our endless journey.

Awaken Your Divine Light

Begin awakening your own Divine light by sitting quietly and simply looking at the cover of this book uninterrupted for at least five minutes. You will find yourself being brought into a deeply relaxed state and then notice what you feel...That feeling is the God-in-you slowly waking up from its lifelong slumber.

To learn more about Jacqueline Ripstein and experience more of her artwork, go to her website at: *www.Godslight.com*

From Illusion to Reality

An Evening of Reality

Spend an evening each month with Andrew Moss and Mark Tosoni, a contributing writer for Andrew's *Monthly Guide for Improving Your Life,* and get a greater glimpse of *"Reality"* as they discuss the topics you definitely want to know more about in "REAL TALK – *An Evening of Reality."* Each intimate monthly conversation will allow you to delve deeper into the principles of creation that affect your life at every moment. Listen in on the conversation as if you were in the room with them as they spend one hour discussing important topics and share information that they do not cover each month in the *Monthly Guide for Improving Your Life.*

The key to changing your life is *"repetition."* The more you are exposed to this new **life-changing** information, the more likely you are to change the habits that will lead to the life you've always desired. Stay plugged in to the Power of the Universe by listening to a new conversation each month.

Listen to a tape:

- While driving to work each morning and activate your "Spiritual Armor" which will protect you for the rest of the day.
- While driving home from work each evening to connect back with your Source and dissolve the negative energy you picked up during a hard day's work.
- Before you go to bed each night to activate your "higher self" and raise your consciousness while you sleep.

Each tape is $9.95 but if you subscribe to our monthly tape program, you will receive a new tape each month for only $7.95, as well as a complimentary 12-cassette album to store 1 year of tapes.

How To Order

Books:

Phone:	Toll-Free (866) 4-REAL-00 (473-2500)
Fax:	Toll-Free (866) 4-REAL-77 (473-2577)
On-line:	www.fromillusiontoreality.com
Mail:	From Illusion To Reality
	6901 W. Okeechobee Blvd. #D-5/334
	West Palm Beach, FL 33411
Price:	Books are $25 (plus S & H*)
Payment:	*By Mail*: Check/Money Order (payable to From Illusion to Reality), VISA, MasterCard, American Express
	By Phone, Fax, On-line & International orders: VISA, MasterCard, American Express

Tapes:

Phone:	Toll-Free (866) 4-REAL-99 (473-2599)
Fax:	Toll-Free (866) 4-REAL-77 (473-2577)
On-line:	www.fromillusiontoreality.com
Mail:	same as above
Price:	Tapes are $9.95 each or only $7.95 each if you sign up for our Monthly Tape Program (plus S & H**)
Payment:	*By Mail*: Check/Money Order (payable to From Illusion to Reality), VISA, MasterCard, American Express
	By Phone, Fax, On-line & International orders: VISA, MasterCard, American Express

FREE Monthly Guide for Improving Your Life (Newsletter):

Printed version only available in U.S. – E-mail version available everywhere

Phone:	Toll-Free (866) 4-REAL-99 (473-2599)
Fax:	Toll-Free (866) 4-REAL-77 (473-2577)
On-line:	www.fromillusiontoreality.com
Mail:	same as above
Price:	FREE

Shipping & Handling (books):	$3.99 - first item
	$ .99 - each additional item
	(Additional for International orders)
**Shipping & Handling (tapes)*:	$1.99 - first item
	$ .99 - each additional item
	(Additional for International orders)